Fascist Italy

Fascist Italy is a lively and concise introduction to the phenomenon of Italian fascism and its impact. The author balances an up-to-date re-evaluation of political, diplomatic and military developments with a full assessment of the more neglected domestic and cultural dimensions of the subject.

With the aid of documents and the latest research, this book presents a clear analysis of the origins of the movement, the reasons behind its political success and the methods used to construct and consolidate a regime capable of resolving the problems of mass society in the twentieth century.

Within his broad-ranging analysis, John Whittam places particular emphasis on the attempts to exert social control, the interaction of party and state, the tension between revolutionary and conservative tendencies and the role of Il Duce. Mussolini's triumphs and failures in peace and war and his ultimate responsibility for the disintegration of the regime are discussed with the objectivity they deserve.

John Whittam is Senior Lecturer in History at the University of Bristol.

NEW FRONTIERS IN HISTORY

series editors

Mark Greengrass
Department of History, Sheffield University

John Stevenson
Worcester College, Oxford

This important new series reflects the substantial expansion that has occurred in the scope of history syllabuses. As new subject areas have emerged and syllabuses have come to focus more upon methods of historical enquiry and knowledge of source materials, a growing need has arisen for correspondingly broad-ranging textbooks.

New Frontiers in History provides up-to-date overviews of key topics in British, European and world history, together with accompanying source material and appendices. Authors focus upon subjects where revisionist work is being undertaken, providing a fresh viewpoint welcomed by students and sixth-formers. The series also explores established topics which have attracted much conflicting analysis and require a synthesis of the state of the debate.

Published titles

C. J. Bartlett Defence and diplomacy: Britain and the Great Powers, 1815–1914

Jeremy Black The politics of Britain, 1688–1800

David Brooks The age of upheaval: Edwardian politics, 1899–1914

Conan Fischer The rise of the Nazis

Keith Laybourn The General Strike of 1926

Panikos Panayi Immigration, ethnicity and racism in Britain, 1815–1945

Daniel Szechi The Jacobites: Britain and Europe, 1688–1788

Forthcoming titles

Paul Bookbinder The Weimar Republic

Joanna Bourke Production and reproduction: working women in Britain, 1860–1960

Michael Braddick The nerves of state: taxation and the financing of the English state, 1558–1714

Ciaran Brady The unplanned conquest: social changes and political conflict in sixteenth-century Ireland

David Carlton Churchill and the Soviets

Carl Chinn Poverty amidst prosperity: the urban poor in England, 1834–1914

Barry Coward The Cromwellian Protectorate

Neville Kirk The rise of Labour, 1850–1920

Tony Kushner The Holocaust and its aftermath

Alan O'Day Irish Home Rule

Contents

Acknowledgements	*page*	vii
List of abbreviations		ix
Introduction		1
1 The formation of the Fascist movement		**6**
The first Fascist meeting		6
The leader		10
Post-war economic and political problems		16
The 'Fascists of the first hour'		19
2 Expansion and breakthrough, 1920–1922		**25**
The challenge of D'Annunzio		25
Squadrismo: the Fascist offensive		28
The March on Rome		34
3 Transition: from coalition to regime, 1922–1928		**41**
A government which governs		41
The entry of the Nationalists		45
The Matteotti crisis		47
The establishment of the Fascist regime		52
4 The construction of the regime: economic		
and social developments		**58**
The Decennale of 1932		58
Economic policy		60
Social reforms		65
Education and youth movements		66
Women		71
Dopolavoro		73

Contents

The Lateran Pacts   75

**5 The search for an ideology: intellectuals,
propaganda and racism**   81
    The Manifesto of the Fascist intellectuals, 21 April 1925   81
    Romanità   85
    Propaganda   88
    Racism   95

6 Diplomacy, war and collapse   101
    Foreign policy: the quiet years, 1922–35   101
    Ethiopia   110
    The Axis   115
    War and defeat   121
    The coup of July 1943 and its consequences   128

Epilogue: the legacy   137

Selected documents   143

Bibliographical essay   168

Index   173

Acknowledgements

The author and publishers would like to thank the following for permission to reproduce the extracts indicated below:

Selected excerpts from *Mediterranean Fascism 1919–1945* by Charles F. Delzell. Copyright 1970 by Charles F. Delzell. Reprinted by permission of HarperCollins Publishers, Inc.

Passages from Renzo de Felice *Mussolini il rivoluzionario* (1965); *Mussolini il Duce*, i (1974) and *Mussolini il Duce*, ii (1981); and from A. Acquarone *L'organizzazione dello stato totalitario* (1965). Reprinted by permission of Guilio Einaudi Editore S.p.A.

Extracts from the Futurist Manifesto taken from J. Joll *Intellectuals in Politics* (1960), by permission of Weidenfeld and Nicolson.

Extracts from A. Lyttleton *Italian Fascisms from Pareto to Gentile* (1973). Reprinted by permission of the Peters Fraser & Dunlop Group Ltd.

Extracts from the Lateran Pacts from J. Pollard *The Vatican and Italian Fascism* (1985), by permission of Cambridge University Press.

Extracts from A. Rossi *Rise of Italian Fascism* (1938), by permission of Methuen & Co.

Extracts from P. Togliatti *Lectures on Fascism* (1976), reprinted by permission of Lawrence and Wishart Ltd.

Acknowledgements

Extracts from *Christ Stopped at Eboli* by Carlo Levi and translated by Frances Frenaye Lanza. Translation copyright © 1947 by Farrar, Straus and Company and renewed © 1974 by Farrar, Straus and Giroux, Inc. Reprinted by permission of Farrar, Straus and Giroux, Inc.

Abbreviations

ANI	*Associazone Nazionale Italiana*
CGL	*Confederazione Generale del Lavoro*
CISNAL	*Confederazione Italiana Sindacati Nazionali Lavoratori*
CLN	*Comitati di Liberazione Nazionale*
DC	*Democrazia Cristiana*
ECCI	*Executive Committee of the Communist International*
EUR	*Esposizione Universale di Roma*
FUCI	*Federazione Universitari Cattolici Italiani*
GIL	*Gioventù Italiana del Littorio*
GUF	*Gioventù Universitaria Fascista/Gruppi Universitari Fascisti*
IMI	*Istituto per la Ricostruzione Industriale*
IRI	*Istituto Mobiliare Italiano*
LUCE	*L'Unione Cinematografica Educativa*
MVSN	*Milizia Voluntaria per la Sicurezza Nazionale*
ONB	*Opera Nazionale Balilla*
OND	*Opera Nazionale Dopolavoro*
ONMI	*Opera Nazionale di Maternità ed Infanzia*
OVRA	*Opera Volontaria per la Repressione Antifascista*
PCd'I	*Partito Comunista d'Italia*
PNF	*Partito Nazionale Fascista*
PPI	*Partito Popolare Italiano*
PSI	*Partito Socialista Italiano*
URI	*Unione Radiofonica Italiana*

Introduction

It has been convincingly argued that attempting to define fascism is like searching for a black cat in a dark and possibly empty room.[1] Despite all the books and the theories, the existence of something called 'European Fascism' or even 'Fascism in Europe' is very hard to prove. Mussolini was right to assert in the 1920s that Italian Fascism was not for export as it was firmly rooted in the national soil. He was wrong when he changed his mind in the early 1930s and affirmed that Fascism 'as idea, doctrine and realisation is universal' and proclaimed that the twentieth century would be the century of facism 'in which Italy for the third time will return to being the guide for human civilisation'.[2] The ludicrous attempt (see p. 107) to establish a Fascist International at Montreux in 1934 finally convinced him to abandon universal Fascism and to recognise once again the unique character of the movement which he had led since March 1919. Interestingly, he had been most reluctant to sanction any official definition of Fascism and only did so in 1932. The reason for this is quite clear: just as European or universal Fascism were illusory ideas, so was the concept of Italian Fascism. Such a concept was perfectly acceptable for the regime's philosopher Giovanni Gentile, for the propagandists, for the School of Fascist Mysticism and for social scientists, but as a practical politician Mussolini knew better.

There were, in reality, several different *Fascisms*. This is one of the themes running through the first three chapters of this book. Even the early Fascists, the 'Fascists of the first hour', were a

1

volatile mixture of ex-socialists, syndicalists, Futurists and war veterans; the *squadristi* who terrorised the countryside after 1920 certainly lacked homogeneity, and their leaders, the *ras*, often hated each other as much as their socialist enemies. The fusion with the Nationalists in 1923 and the adhesion to the party of conservative businessmen and Catholics made it increasingly difficult to determine the character and aims of Fascism. As Giuseppe Bottai, one of the shrewdest Fascist leaders, explained the problem: the various Fascisms had triumphantly marched on Rome in October 1922 and now the major task was to construct Fascism. Writing in Bottai's journal *Critica Fascista* Augusto De Marsanich commented on the mystical unity which had held the disparate groups together 'but when reality forces us to pass from the heroic and religious period to the political and critical, this unity collapses and *our party is revealed as a mosaic*. Today only the intellect and will of Mussolini can still control and direct us'. De Marsanich identified the major defect of the party as 'the absence of an organic and clearly defined central idea'. Both liberalism and Marxism possessed a distinct ideology but, he continued, 'there is no Fascist political doctrine other than the concept of the Nation hierarchically organised . . . and this is revealed by the multiplicity of interpretations made by Fascists themselves so that *each individual believes in his own type of Fascism*'.[3] This has been extensively quoted because it is such an important statement outlining the problem of analysing Italian Fascism.

Opponents of Fascism found it equally difficult to comprehend. Communists of the Third International like Karl Radek observed the crucial significance of the lower middle classes, who saw themselves threatened by Big Business from above and the trade unions from below and sought salvation by pursuing a 'middle way' between capitalism and socialism.[4] By the late 1920s, however, the official Communist line accused the entire bourgeois class of being Fascist, only to change again in the mid-1930s. 'Fascism is the open, terrorist dictatorship of the most reactionary, most chauvinist and most imperialist elements of finance capital' was the next and most famous definition – Fascism as the dying kick of a doomed capitalism.[5] Like so many liberals, the philosopher Benedetto Croce saw Fascism as an invigorating new force which could be usefully integrated into the political system. He changed his mind after 1924 and

2

described it as an aberration, a 'parenthesis' or a kind of mental breakdown which afflicted Italians and other Europeans in the inter-war period. Philosophically and historically this was an unconvincing interpretation.[6] Equally unsatisfactory appears to be the view that Fascism was a modernising dictatorship in an underdeveloped country.[7] The same is true of the opposing theory that it was anti-industrial and anti-modernisation. These 'developmental theories' are interesting but largely irrelevant to the study of Fascist Italy.

It is not modernisation but mobilisation which is relevant. The mobilisation of the masses and the imposition of social controls are major themes in the third and fourth chapters of this book, and it is no coincidence that the first document provides extracts from Gustave Le Bon's *The Crowd*, a book which intrigued and influenced Mussolini (see Document 1). The political mobilisation of the masses is supposed to have begun with the French Revolution, the economic mobilisation with the Industrial Revolution and total mobilisation for war between 1914 and 1918. The advance of democracy, socialism and trade unionism was regarded apprehensively by conservatives, who responded with repressive legislation, police actions and a military presence. Liberals acted more imaginatively by combining a flexible approach to law and order with a programme of cautious political and social reforms. Prime Ministers Francesco Crispi and General Luigi Pelloux represented the cruder conservative approach in the 1890s, prime Minister Giovanni Giolitti the more sophisticated liberal response of the early 1900s. Mussolini and his followers rejected liberalism and regarded the defensive conservatism of the old elites as totally inadequate, especially after the experience of the war and the Bolshevik Revolution. Using nationalism as their ideological weapon and paramilitary formations to impose their views, they embarked on an ambitious and vigorous programme of consensus building. Clubs and castor oil played a significant part in the initial phases and helped Mussolini to secure the premiership in 1922, but with the consolidation of the regime after the mid-1920s social control over a mass society was achieved by an impressive series of innovatory measures. The simultaneous mobilisation and depoliticisation of Italian society was a remarkable *tour de force*, matched only by the progressive political emasculation of the Fascist Party itself.[8]

3

These efforts at social control – largely effective until the late 1930s – involved the relationship between party and state, between state and church, educational and youth policies, the conduct of propaganda, the organisation of leisure and the concept of the corporative state. It is in this area that some of the most stimulating research into Fascist Italy has been carried out over the last two decades. The names of these historians are recorded in the notes and in the bibliography rather than in the text itself. It is hoped that readers will not find this peculiarity too disturbing.

This book concentrates on providing a balanced account of Fascist Italy rather than discussing the various interpretations of Fascism. The first three chapters are largely chronological in approach, analysing the various strands within the Fascist movement, and explaining the reasons for the successful March on Rome and the consolidation of power in the following years. The next two chapters are more thematic and deal with the most important characteristics of Fascist Italy. The final chapter traces the course of foreign policy which eventually brought about the collapse of the regime. The epilogue deals specifically with the neo-Fascists. There were, of course, many other important consequences of the Fascist era, but their examination would require another book to be written.

The name of Mussolini occurs several times on nearly every page of this book. Implicitly or explicitly the 'cult of the Duce' is a dominant theme. For Mussolini Fascism was more a means than an end. Bottai complained that it was the Duce who prevented the realisation of Fascism in Italy; it was, after all, 'Mussolini's Italy', but it must be remembered that millions of Italians, actively or passively, encouraged and supported its creation. In a broadcast to the Italian people on 23 December 1940 Winston Churchill said: 'That he is a great man I do not deny, but that after eighteen years of unbridled power he has led your country to the horrid verge of ruin can be denied by none'. In a famous phrase he proclaimed that 'one man, and one man alone' was responsible for the destiny of Italy.[9] At the time this was good propaganda, but as a political leader and as a historian Churchill knew this to be false. Three years later over forty million Italians wanted it to be true.

Introduction

Notes

1 G. Allardyce, 'What fascism is not: thoughts on the deflation of a concept', *American Historical Review*, 84, 2, 1979, p. 368.

2 M. Ledeen, *Universal Fascism*, New York, 1972, is most useful on this theme.

3 *Critica Fascista*, 15 December 1923; my italics.

4 R. De Felice, *Le Interpretazioni del fascismo*, Bari, 1976, pp. 69–70. See also L. Salvatorelli, *Nazionalfascismo*, Turin, 1923. He wrote that the petty bourgeoisie was placed between Big Business and the proletariat like a third man between two fighters.

5 *Theses and Decisions of the Third Plenum of the ECCI*, London, 1934, contains the views of the Comintern prior to their congress of 1935, as expressed in the Executive Committee of the Communist International (ECCI).

6 De Felice, *Le Interpretazioni*, pp. 235–7.

7 A. Organski, 'Fascism and modernisation', in S. Woolf (ed.), *The Nature of Fascism*, London, 1968.

8 A fine introduction to this is P. Melograni, 'The cult of the Duce in Mussolini's Italy', *Journal of Contemporary History*, 11, 4, 1976.

9 M. Gilbert, *Finest Hour: Winston S. Churchill 1939–41*, London, 1983, p. 960.

1

The formation of the Fascist movement

The first Fascist meeting

Fascism was the name adopted by a hundred or so men and a handful of women who assembled in a hall on the Piazza San Sepolcro in Milan on 23 March 1919. The date, the place and these *sansepolcristi* all became part of the 'sacred lore' of the pseudo-religion of fascism which developed in the next two decades. This first *fascio italiano di combattimento* (Italian combat group) had been summoned by Mussolini through the pages of his newspaper *Il Popolo d'Italia*. The term 'Fascism' was, of course, derived from *fascio*; it simply meant members of this particular group. *Fascio* was, in turn, derived from the Latin word fasces, the bundle of rods containing an axe carried by the lictor (*littorio* in Italian) in ancient Rome as a symbol of authority. It soon became the all-pervasive symbol of Fascist Italy as the regime strove to recreate the power and prestige of the Roman Empire. If Fascism was a new addition to the political lexicon of the twentieth century and soon to become depressingly familiar, the word *fascio* was already well-established. Garibaldi had founded one, left-wing Sicilians had created *fasci* in the early 1890s, and between 1914 and 1919 numerous *fasci* had been organised by interventionists, Futurists, Nationalist deputies, volunteers and *arditi*, the elite commando troops who had operated behind enemy lines in the First World War. None of them, however, appear to have called themselves Fascists. Those who decided to join Mussolini's movement during the months following 23 March 1919 became the proud bearers of the title 'Fascists of the first hour'. Their specific beliefs and aims were less important than their loyal support for the new

6

movement and its leader Benito Mussolini.

At the first meeting in Milan the *arditi* were very much in evidence and one of their leaders, Ferruccio Vecchi, actually presided over the proceedings. Nevertheless, it was Mussolini who made the keynote speeches and dominated the assembly. Similar scenes were enacted throughout Europe in the turbulent year of 1919 with fanatical orators haranguing receptive audiences, but what distinguished this meeting from all the others was that this particular orator became prime minister of his country within four years and established a regime which lasted for more than twenty years. The programme that he proposed was a radical one, dealing briefly with several aspects of the political, social and economic life of the nation. With some alterations, it formed the basis of the official manifesto of early fascism published on 6 June 1919 (see Document 2). As in all his speeches prior to the March on Rome in October 1922, Mussolini made it abundantly clear that his prime aim was the seizure of power: 'The right to the political succession belongs to us because it was we who forced the country into the war and led it to victory'.[1] He condemned all political parties and it was only in the autumn of 1921 that he finally decided to allow his movement to become the National Fascist Party (PNF). Contemptuous of parliament and the corrupt and inefficient liberals who had ruled Italy for so long, Mussolini called for a new ruling elite who would sweep away the old system and establish a 'new order' in Italy. His attacks on the liberals who had supported Giovanni Giolitti before and during the war were bitter enough, but he positively excoriated his former comrades in the Socialist Party not because they supported the workers' demands but because they had opposed intervention in 1914–15. This was, after all, the basic issue which had led to his expulsion from the party. 'We declare war on socialism not because it is socialist but because it has opposed nationalism'. Indeed, Mussolini declared his support for the eight-hour day, sickness and old-age insurance, workers' control over industry and the economic programme put forward by the National Syndicalists – provided the emphasis was placed on national unity and not on class division. He also mentioned the possibility of organising corporations and setting up 'occupational councils'. The questions of syndicalism and corporativism were to be endlessly debated over the next twenty years,

7

Mussolini's attitude towards both becoming increasingly sceptical.

The political programme accepted by this first Fascist meeting included universal suffrage for men and women (although votes for women rapidly ran into difficulties), proportional representation and the election of a constituent assembly. This assembly would determine whether Italy became a republic or remained a monarchy, and Mussolini advocated republicanism. The abolition of the senate was also proposed but, like republicanism, was later abandoned. It was clear that, despite their anti-parliamentarianism, the Fascists intended to become involved in traditional politics as well as engaging in various forms of direct action, such as street violence or the sacking of the offices of *Avanti!*, the Socialist newspaper, which took place in mid-April 1919.

Mussolini had warned his audience of the evils of Bolshevism in Russia and its possible expansion westwards, a theme which he pursued relentlessly for the rest of his life and which became an invaluable propaganda weapon. His main targets were, of course, the Marxist parties of Italy: the Socialists (PSI) and later the Communists (the PCd'I, which emerged in January 1921). But if anti-Marxism served the Fascists well, anticlericalism proved less effective. Mussolini and most of the early Fascists were notoriously hostile to the church, the papacy and religion itself and had included confiscation of religious property in their June 1919 programme. There was another reason for their hostility towards Catholics. In January 1919 the Populist Party, the *Partito Popolare Italiano* (PPI), had been founded by the Sicilian priest Luigi Sturzo and by the end of the year the new party had a mass following, becoming a powerful political competitor of both the Socialists and the Fascists. Within two years, however, Fascist attacks on the church became less frequent as it was increasingly apparent that the ecclesiastical hierarchy and many Catholics saw Fascism as an indispensable counterforce not only to Marxism but also to the leftist elements in the PPI. This was certainly how the new Pope Pius XI read the situation after his election in 1922. It was a development which anticlerical Fascists viewed with deep distaste but which their leader reluctantly endorsed.

At this first Fascist meeting Catholics, Socialists and Giolittian liberals were attacked because of their lack of patriotism before, during, and after the war. Mussolini and his followers glorified the war, the heroism of the troops and the 'solidarity of the trenches', by which they meant the cameraderie of officers and men on the front line as they faced death at the hands of the enemy. This was an experience which the civilians of the home front could never fully understand. With four million soldiers being demobilised in 1919, Mussolini quickly realised the need to recruit as many of them as possible into his movement. Because of war weariness and the suspiciousness of the peasant ex-combatants, the Fascists were not immediately successful but the Socialists played into their hands by treating the veterans with disrespect, accusing them of being dupes and class traitors. Even though most of them voted for the Socialists or Populists in the November 1919 elections, many of them continued to feel great resentment at the way in which their war service had been devalued and were thus tempted into the ranks of the Fascists. The Socialists' loss was the Fascists' gain. But it was the officer class which became the main target of abuse by the left-wing parties.

Mussolini's attitude to the regular army was always somewhat ambivalent. In the Fascist programme of 1919 the creation of a National Militia was demanded, together with the nationalisation of all armaments factories. It was assumed that the militia would become a peoples' army and displace the royal army. The Fascists did, indeed, set up their *squadre d'azione* (action squads) and in 1923 these were largely incorporated into the Militia or MVSN (Voluntary Militia for National Security), but the regular army remained untouched and still owed allegiance to King Victor Emmanuel III. The rise of Fascism and the consolidation of the regime owed much to the neutrality or active support of the army. As Mussolini realised, only by abandoning republicanism could the movement avoid confrontation with the royalist officer corps. This 'conversion' was publicly announced in September 1922, just a few weeks prior to the March on Rome (see Document 3).

By the autumn of 1922 the initial programme of the Fascists had been drastically revised. Republicanism, anticlericalism and criticism of the army had ceased to be part of their official propaganda; so too had the abolition of the Senate, votes for women and various discriminatory taxes on war profits. Increasingly the emphasis was placed on nationalism, an active foreign policy and a strong, authoritarian state. To achieve this the Fascists called upon the youthful, dynamic forces of Italy to rally round their movement and sweep away the pernicious influence of liberalism, Marxism and Sturzo's Populists. A strong leader was required to create a strong state and Mussolini claimed that role for himself.

The leader

Mussolini was born in Predappio in the Romagna in 1883, and it has been argued that his place of birth was perhaps 'the major influence in determining his character'.[2] It was true that for centuries the Romagna was regarded as one of the most turbulent regions in the peninsula, but there were three much more formative influences on the early life of Mussolini. These were his father, his schooling, and his two visits just beyond the borders of Italy first to Switzerland and then to the Austrian Trentino. From his father Alessandro, the socialist blacksmith, he received the names Benito, Amilcare, Andrea (Benito Juarez was the Mexican revolutionary, Amilcare Cipriani and Andrea Costa were Italian socialists) and an abiding passion for the politics of violence. At his school in Faenza where the poor sat at separate tables and ate inferior food, he gained personal experience of social divisions. Forty years later he still remembered the shame he had felt.[3] This bitterness towards the privileged classes resurfaced many times during his period of power and especially after 1943. In the small world of Faenza the young Benito had encountered some of the main problems confronting the whole of Italy. There was the enormous gap which separated the mass of the people from the privileged minority, who had constructed a United Italy and controlled its destiny for more than a generation. There was also the tension between church and state reflected in the attitude of the Salesian brothers who taught Mussolini, and whose rigid intolerance fed his rebelliousness and stimulated his anti-clericalism. Even schoolchildren were aware of the disparity between the rich and the poor, the town and the countryside; with their regional accents or dialects, their own specific customs and historical memories, most of them acquired only a thin veneer of *italianità* (the awareness of belonging to a specific,

Italian cultural society) and few of them, outside the ranks of the gentry and the established middle classes, had any clear concept of Italian nationalism.

Indeed, while Mussolini was a teenager in the 1890s, liberal Italy appeared to be disintegrating. Two attempts were made to stabilise the state, reassert the authority of government, and resolve the problems which liberalism had failed to confront effectively. The first was by Prime Minister Francesco Crispi, a former follower of Garibaldi and a man who aspired to become the Bismarck of Italy. In the mid-1890s when conciliation broke down, Crispi pursued a ruthless policy of police repression to defeat the subversive *fasci* in his native Sicily and to smash the socialists and trade unionists in the northern cities. This rather old-fashioned authoritarianism in the domestic sphere was accompanied by an ambitious foreign and colonial policy which attempted to assert Italy's great power status. Crispi's dream of empire in Africa was shattered by the defeat of Adua in 1896 at the hands of Ethiopian tribesmen, a disaster which Mussolini was to avenge in 1935. Crispi had failed to become the strong man of Italy and was driven from power. *Italia* seemed doomed to remain *Italietta* (little Italy). The second attempt to assert state authority was made by General Pelloux in the last years of the decade. In 1897 Sidney Sonnino had written an article which became something of a sacred text for conservatives and reactionaries. His 'Return to the Constitution' ('*Torniamo allo Statuto*') called for the strengthening of the executive, the king and his ministers, at the expense of parliament. As the fiftieth anniversary of the great 1848 revolutions approached and as economic distress was matched by increasing political agitation, a frightened government called in the army, which proclaimed martial law in Milan, shot eighty civilians and made mass arrests. In June 1898 General Pelloux was appointed prime minister and for a year he attempted to calm the situation, to reconcile order with liberty, but Sonnino's ideas became increasingly attractive and Pelloux submitted to parliament a draconian coercion bill which would have curtailed basic liberties. Throughout June 1899 the opposition in parliament blocked the bill and the sitting ended in chaos at the end of the month.[4] From November 1899, when parliament reassembled, until June 1900 Italy came perilously close to becoming an authoritarian regime. Ironically,

11

it was the decision of Pelloux and Sonnino to challenge their liberal and left-wing opponents by holding new elections that led to what has been called a 'crushing moral defeat' and the resignation of Pelloux in June 1900.[5] Liberal Italy had survived, but only just. The assassination of King Humbert the following month had the curious effect of uniting Italians and inaugurating a period of progress and stability dominated by Giovanni Giolitti.

These two traditionalist and rather half-hearted attempts to create a more authoritarian Italian state are worth recording because it was Mussolini who made the third attempt in the early 1920s. He succeeded where Crispi and Pelloux had failed, realising that the new 'age of the masses' required a new approach and new techniques (see Document 1). Fascist Italy was the result. But at the turn of the century the young Mussolini was embarking on a brief and disastrous career as a schoolteacher. He found his true vocation after emigrating to Switzerland. This move was prompted by his need to seek employment and to distance himself from various domestic complications, including the requirement to perform his military service. The influence of his father and his experiences at school and elsewhere had already made him a radical; his sojourn in Switzerland converted him to socialism. Socialists helped him after his first spell in prison and encouraged him to write articles and make speeches. The Russian émigré Angelica Balabanov tried unsuccessfully to ensure that he acquired a solid grasp of Marxist theory, and the Italian leader Giacinto Serrati acted as his patron and helped him to rise rapidly within the socialist movement. Taking advantage of an amnesty, Mussolini returned to Italy to undergo his military service in 1904. Surprisingly, he seemed to relish the discipline of army life. He decided after his release to re-enter the teaching profession, but once again this proved a fiasco. His socialist contacts found him a post as newspaper editor in the Austrian Trentino. So for several months in 1909 he once again lived beyond the northern borders of Italy and this time he was not imprisoned for begging. He came into contact with irredentists, Italians who claimed that the Trentino, Trieste and other areas within the Habsburg Monarchy should be incorporated into Italy, but as a socialist he remained aloof from this nationalist agitation. What the Austrian authorities disliked most about Mussolini was his strident anticlericalism and this was why they expelled him in September 1909. As a result, he became something of a revolutionary hero.

His residence in Switzerland and the Trentino was important for three reasons. He found his true vocation as a talented political agitator, a brilliant journalist and a most effective orator. Secondly, he made contact with a wide network of socialists and other subversives, which improved his career prospects within the Socialist Party, but he also read the articles of right-wing nationalists and corresponded with men like Giuseppe Prezzolini. Thirdly, it made him aware of the shameful treatment meted out to Italians living abroad, how they were mercilessly exploited and treated with contempt even in such an enlightened country as Switzerland. Already conscious of class divisions and having an inferiority complex as a result, Mussolini realised that he and the Italians as a race were regarded as inferior, a nation of illiterate peasants, manual labourers, waiters, barbers and tourist guides. Mussolini came to share this national inferiority complex and later sought to exorcise it.

In the four years after 1910, Mussolini became one of the most outstanding leaders of the intransigent wing of the PSI, first on the local level in his native Romagna as editor of *La Lotte di Classe* (class struggle), and then on the national level as editor of the party's official newspaper *Avanti!* in 1912. This promotion was the result of his vitriolic attacks on the reformists in the party at their congress in Reggio Emilia in July. He had already been imprisoned for his attempts to sabotage Italy's colonial war in Libya, and at the congress he had been assigned the task of driving out of the party all those, like the moderate Socialist Leonida Bissolati, who had become reformist collaborators of Prime Minister Giolitti. As a leader of the revolutionary socialists who seized control of the party, he was in his element launching attacks on the Giolittian liberals and revisionist socialists. During 'Red Week' in June 1914, which followed the party's congress at Ancona two months previously, Italy seemed close to a revolutionary transformation and activists like Mussolini seemed poised to seize power. It was, however, an illusion, as the strike movement and disturbances remained localised in the Marches and Umbria. Even if war had not broken out in August 1914 there would not have been an Italian revolution, but at the time people were not so sure.

The outbreak of the First World War presented Mussolini and the government with the first of many dilemmas. Since 1882 Italy had been the partner of Germany and Austria-Hungary in the Triple Alliance, but in recent years she had moved closer to the Triple Entente of Britain, France and Russia. As Vienna had not kept Rome informed about her reaction to the assassination of Franz Ferdinand and her determination to humiliate Serbia, Italy was not obliged to go to war in support of the central powers. The decision to remain neutral was welcomed by supporters of Giolitti (who had left office in March but still controlled a large following in parliament), by the Vatican and most Catholics and by the Socialists. The peasant masses, whose sons provided cannon-fodder in any war, were also opposed to war. So, at first, was Mussolini. For two months he loyally followed the official party line but became increasingly frustrated by Italy's inaction. On 18 October 1914 he wrote an editorial in *Avanti!* advocating intervention on the side of the Entente. If he had hoped to swing the party in this direction he was sadly mistaken. His horrified comrades swiftly dismissed him from his editorial post and expelled him from the party. From November 1914 Mussolini was an ex-Socialist and he never forgave the PSI for its treatment of him and for its failure to see that the 'revolutionary war' against the militaristic and reactionary central powers was an opportunity not to be missed. On 15 November 1914 he was able to support the interventionist movement in the pages of his new newspaper *Il Popolo d'Italia*, financed partly by funds provided by Italians like Filippo Naldi (the conservative editor of another newspaper *Il Resto del Carlino*) and partly by the French government.

The opponent of the Libyan war had become an ardent supporter of Italian involvement in a vast European war. The man who seemed destined to become the leader of an extremist Socialist party was now an outcast with only a newspaper and a few friends; ostracised by the left and suspected by the right, his political career appeared to be over. Like many interventionists he joined one of the *fasci di azione rivoluzionaria*, which were spearheaded by revolutionary syndicalists like A.O. Olivetti, Filippo Corridoni, Michele Bianchi and Cesare Rossi. Several of them became close associates of Mussolini over the next few years. Although there were only around 9,000 members they played an important part in the street demonstrations and rallies which preceded Italy's entry into the war. As the name of these groups indicated, they were engaged in 'revolutionary action' and equated war with revolution; they also threatened the government with revolution if it failed to respond to their demands. *Il Popolo d'Italia* became their mouthpiece. Their finest hour was during 'Radiant May' in 1915 when they helped to frighten the Giolittian deputies in parliament into voting for war.[6] Mussolini dated the eventual success of his movement from this humiliation of parliament, involving the defeat of the neutralists and defeatists in the ranks of the liberals, Socialists and Catholics. Less justifiably, he did tend to foster the impression that he and the interventionist *fasci* played the key role in forcing the declaration of war. This ignored the fact that it was the poet and novelist Gabriele D'Annunzio who attracted most attention, and that the government of Antonio Salandra (prime minister March 1914–June 1916) and the king had already signed the secret Treaty of London with the Entente on 26 April 1915. In any case, pressure groups dominated by the Nationalists of the *Associazione nazionale italiano* (the ANI had been founded in 1910 by Enrico Corradini and Luigi Federzoni) were far more influential than the *fasci*. The latter were, in fact, dissolved on the outbreak of war and the interventionists, including Mussolini, joined the armed forces to fight the Austrians. At least they practised what they preached.

Mussolini joined his unit in August 1915 and remained in the army until invalided out in the summer of 1917. He spent six months at the front, proved to be a disciplined and courageous soldier and was promoted to the rank of corporal. He witnessed at first hand the so-called 'spirit of the trenches' or *trincerismo* of the front-line troops; this comradeship (perhaps most realistically portrayed by Henri Barbusse in *Under Fire*) often persisted into peacetime and played an important part in the formation of ex-combatant associations; the role of the *arditi* in the first phase of fascism has already been noted.[7] By October 1917, when the Italian front caved in at Caporetto, Mussolini was back at his editorial desk in Milan. He blamed the political elite and the defeatist socialists for this military defeat. The Austro-German advance into northern Italy led to a genuine outburst of patriotism among ordinary Italians and to keep the soldiers in the line the government made many rash promises, including land for the peasants in uniform and the Italian equivalent of Lloyd George's 'homes fit for heroes'. This raised hopes, and when they were not fulfilled after 1918 an ugly mood of resentment developed which could be manipulated by agitators of the left or the right. As the Habsburg Monarchy collapsed in 1918, the Italian army was able to assume the offensive and win the battle of Vittorio Veneto on 30 October 1918, just before the signing of the Austro-Italian armistice on 4 November.

The neutralist controversy of 1914-15 and the war experience of 1915-18 were of crucial significance for Mussolini and the fascist movement. They also created fresh divisions in an already disunited Italy. But equally important was the debate over the peace settlement. The Treaty of London had promised Italy her unredeemed lands to the north, a long stretch of the Adriatic coastline and colonial gains in Africa and Anatolia. Fiume, a seaport to the east of the Istrian peninsula had not been included. Despite the creation of Yugoslavia technically the kingdom of the Serbs, Croats and Slovenes until 1929 and President Wilson's opposition to Italian claims to Slav territories, the prime minister and foreign minister of Italy, Orlando and Sonnino, insisted on pressing their claims and boycotted the Paris peace conference for a period over the refusal of the other three members of the Big Four to consent to Italy's acquisition of Dalmatia and Fiume. The settlement eventually granted Italy Trieste, the Istrian peninsula, a few points further south on the Adriatic and the Trentino and southern Tyrol; the latter was the home of over 200,000 Germans, and Istria was largely populated by Slovenes and Croats. The Fiume issue remained unresolved and this, together with other 'failures' at the conference, prompted Nationalist protests at the 'mutilated victory' and increasing criticism of a parliamentary system which had mishandled the war and now seemed incapable of making a satisfactory peace. Mussolini and his followers were swift to endorse the full programme of the irredentists and the Nationalists.

Post-War economic and political problems

Nationalist hostility towards Italians who favoured concessions to the Slavs of the Adriatic was dramatically revealed on 11

January 1919, when a meeting addressed by Leonida Bissolati at La Scala in Milan was violently disrupted by Mussolini, *arditi* and Futurists. This incident clearly showed the continuity between the street demonstrations of the pre-war interventionists and the terror campaign of the fascists in the post-war period. But there were two important differences. Their war experience had given them greater military expertise and the success of the Bolsheviks in Russia had sharpened their anti-Marxism. On 15 April 1919 they assaulted the newspaper offices of *Avanti!*. It was their first operation after the founding of the *fascio di combattimento* and for Mussolini it was sweet revenge against his former comrades who had expelled him from the Socialist Party and dismissed him as editor. *Fasci* quickly spread to other northern cities outside Milan, but the hard core of activists were spectacularly unsuccessful in attracting new recruits. By the end of 1919 there were less than a thousand members in the movement, clear indication that the rise of fascism was far from inevitable. At first sight, this failure is difficult to understand. It is important, therefore, first to outline the economic and political situation in Italy which seemed to offer such advantages to a movement like Fascism, and then secondly to examine briefly the strengths and weaknesses of these 'Fascists of the first hour'.

For the great majority of Italians in the post-war period it was not foreign policy issues nor political posturing but the deplorable economic situation which they viewed with the gravest concern. Like all the belligerents, Italy's economy and her external trade had been distorted during the war. The 'merchants of death' who supplied the armed forces had made enormous profits, and Mussolini had condemned them in his initial programme and demanded that they be heavily taxed. Farmers had also enjoyed a boom as the price of food rose. The sudden ending of the war, however, the cessation of wartime loans, the abandonment of government controls, the need for industry to revert to peacetime production and the return of four million soldiers, all contributed to an acute economic crisis. Among the demobilised were 130,000 officers, most of them of junior rank, lower middle class, keen to retain the status achieved in the army and determined to continue asserting their authority in the civilian world. It has been estimated that no fewer than 20,000 chose to take courses at university.[8] Soldiers who became students mingled with students who wanted to become soldiers and out of this combustible mixture emerged recruits for the paramilitary formations which fought a civil war over the next few years.

Throughout 1919 the economic situation deteriorated. By November there were two million unemployed, the lira weakened and as inflation took hold wages, pensions and savings were eroded just as the cost of living rose. Food riots and strikes intensified the problem. Industrial workers sought safety by joining trade unions and the membership of the socialist General Confederation of Labour (CGL) rose from 250,000 in 1918 to two million by 1920; Catholic unions claimed over one million and the syndicalists 300,000. In rural areas Socialist and Catholic unions and co-operatives sponsored the occupation of uncultivated land, controlled labour exchanges and *camere di lavoro*, and in the local elections of the autumn of 1920 won control of nearly half of all municipal councils. The government condoned this seizure of land and stood aside during strikes and factory sit-ins, which increasingly infuriated landowners and industrialists. Small, independent farmers and businessmen felt even more vulnerable as the left-wing unions and co-operatives exerted more and more pressure and sought to control wage rates and labour contracts. Central government appeared to have abdicated its responsibilities, so many of those under threat from the 'red menace' looked for support elsewhere.

Between 1918 and 1922 a succession of weak governments had signally failed to solve most of Italy's post-war problems. The last five prime ministers of liberal Italy were Vittorio Emanuele Orlando (until June 1919), Francesco Nitti (June 1919–June 1920), Giovanni Giolitti (June 1920–July 1921), Ivanoe Bonomi (July 1921–February 1922) and Luigi Facta (February 1922–October 1922). Perhaps they do not fully deserve the vicious accusations levelled against them. Apart from Orlando, they were confronted by a new electoral system with proportional representation and the vote extended to all adult males. In the elections of November 1919 two mass parties had emerged, the Socialists of the PSI with 156 seats and the Catholics of the PPI with 100. Together they could have dominated the chamber, but collaboration proved impossible and so they cancelled each other out. In addition, both had internal divisions with radical and reformist wings competing against each other; in January 1921, for instance, the

PSI was weakened by the birth of a new Communist party (PCd'I) and the PPI by incessant calls by the Vatican and right-wing elements to curb the activities of its more democratic members who took 'populism' too literally. The old, liberal ruling elite was also divided between interventionists who had followed Salandra, and neutralists who had supported Giolitti. Nevertheless, the liberals had to construct unstable coalitions because the two mass parties refused to do so. Inevitably such governments were largely unrepresentative of opinion in parliament and in the country. Only if they achieved some outstanding successes would they gain credibility and prevent the disintegration of liberal Italy.

The 'Fascists of the first hour'

Despite the disarray of post-war Italy it took the fascists nearly two years to find enough political space to make any dramatic impact on national life. The decision to enter the elections of 1919 proved unwise. In their stronghold of Milan where Mussolini, Marinetti and Arturo Toscanini were included in their list of candidates, less than 5,000 electors voted for them and no Fascists were elected. Over 70,000 voted for the PPI and 168,000 for the PSI.[9] In Milan and elsewhere this was clearly a vote against war and a vote for the reform programmes of the Socialists and Catholics. The patriotic Fascists with their demagogic demands and their comical candidates had been almost completely ignored. Fascists could draw some slight comfort from two factors. Forty-three per cent of the electorate had failed to vote, which suggested that commitment to parliamentary democracy was not exactly overwhelming and that alternative routes to power might become plausible. Secondly, the parties of the old ruling class had failed to maintain the position they had held in parliament for the last fifty years.

This was, however, scant consolation for the disillusioned Fascists of 1919 and some of them prepared to desert a movement which seemed destined to be ephemeral. It is difficult to categorise these early Fascists. Filippo Tommaso Marinetti, for instance, was simultaneously a Fascist, a leader of the *arditi* and founder and spokesman of Futurism. Many others literally wore different hats and changed the colour of their shirts to produce a dazzling political kaleidoscope. It was Mussolini's daunting task to emphasise the common aims of the disparate groups who joined his *fasci* in 1919 and afterwards. He did not seek to impose complete conformity for three reasons. He might lose their support; indeed, Marinetti and several *arditi* resigned from the *fasci* when the movement appeared to turn towards conservative policies, but Marinetti himself later joined the PNF and remained loyal to the Duce for the rest of his life. Secondly, he wanted to appeal to different sections of the population and so tolerated a certain degree of individuality. Finally, it would be easier to divide and rule if he could play off one faction against another and so keep control of the movement. However, he did insist upon the wearing of the black shirt. This colour was chosen because it was the uniform of the *arditi* and showed the continuity between the movement aﬡd the heroism of the front-line troops during the war. A more mundane reason was the fact that red, white and blue had been pre-empted by Socialists, Catholics and Nationalists and that colours like yellow and green might be misconstrued.

Among the earliest recruits to Fascism were ex-Socialists like Mussolini himself. With their background they hoped to attract a large following from the working classes, to wean them away from the Marxist doctrine of class war and convert them to a form of national socialism. In this they were largely unsuccessful, at least for the first few years. These ex-Socialists had the advantage of knowing the strengths and weaknesses of their former comrades, were well acquainted with the organisation and the personnel of the PSI, and once hostilities had commenced were able to hit them hard where they were most vulnerable. The *arditi*, of course, played a conspicuous role in such punitive operations and their presence among the early fascists requires no further elaboration. Republicans also joined the movement, many of them hoping to complete the task begun by their hero Giuseppe Mazzini during the Risorgimento. They faced a dilemma when fascism abandoned republicanism. Some left the movement but others remained, hoping that the opportunistic Mussolini might turn against the monarchy, which he did, but not until 1943!

The most intriguing and unpredictable of all the early Fascists, however, were Marinetti's Futurists. They had launched themselves upon a startled world with their famous manifesto of 1909 (see Document 4). It had been drawn up by Marinetti and a group of avant-garde artists which included Carlo Carrà, Umberto Boccioni, Luigi Russolo and Gino Severini. Their aim was to shock the bourgeois world out of its complacency, to ridicule established traditions and all orthodox opinions. They extolled the beauty of the new age of technology and the dynamism of the modern world of machines, factories, furnaces and weapons of war. Obsessed by the concepts of speed and motion, they glorified the motor car and the aeroplane. They preached the need for violence and war and became practitioners of both. They delighted in provocative acts, street demonstrations and riotous behaviour, anything to attract attention and create controversy, whether it be about art, politics or foreign policy. As their name indicates, they saw themselves as the heralds of the twentieth century and they attacked all those who were guilty of looking back to the past; these they called the *passatisti* and this was a term which they applied to most Italians. They deplored contemporary Italy, full of museums, archaeologists, tourist guides and second-hand book shops. Venice, Florence and Rome were condemned for living in the past and the reverence for the artistic, literary and architectural heritage of Italy was derided. Demanding the emergence of a powerful, industrialised and warlike nation, the Futurists supported the Libyan war, joined the interventionists in 1914-15 and participated in the war against the central powers. In 1919 they were attracted by fascism and their peculiar talents undoubtedly helped the movement in its early phases. Marinetti hoped that Mussolini would acknowledge their right to cultural hegemony within the movement, but they were too outrageous and volatile and Mussolini was too 'bourgeois' for the partnership to last. Although the future Duce continued to use their expressions in his speeches and writings and although he adopted many of their techniques, after 1920 the Futurists were marginalised. Marinetti himself, the man who led campaigns to abolish academies and museums, was appointed secretary of the fascist writers' union and a member of the *Accademia d'Italia* in 1929.[10] Like Gabriele D'Annunzio, Marinetti was granted an honorary but innocuous position among the luminaries of the fascist regime.

The revolutionary syndicalists formed the final identifiable group to join the early fascists. They had a much sterner attitude to life and Italy's problems than the Futurists and regarded many of Marinetti's antics as deplorable and irrelevant; his advocacy of 'Futurist cooking', for instance, which involved a campaign to prevent the consumption of pasta, was unlikely to arouse their enthusiasm. Revolutionary syndicalists have been described as the 'hard core of early fascism', real professionals with practical knowledge of trade-union activities and long experience of political realities.[11] The syndicalists had broken away from the Socialist Party and its labour movement in 1907. Some of them supported the Libyan war and members of the Nationalist Association (ANI), like Enrico Corradini, hoped to attract them into this new movement. Corradini urged them to abandon class war and to support the concept of Italy as a 'proletarian nation' in conflict with 'plutocratic nations' (see Document 5). For the time being, the syndicalists rejected these appeals. They did, however, become interventionists when the European war broke out and often found themselves working in parallel with Nationalists. Mussolini welcomed their call for a revolutionary war and encouraged them to contribute articles to *Il Popolo d'Italia*. Sergio Panunzio, a leading theorist of syndicalism, began writing for Mussolini's newspaper and continued to do so until his death in 1944. Like many of the other syndicalists, such as Angelo Olivetti and Paolo Orano, Panunzio was an intellectual and not a wild-eyed revolutionary worker. He became a professor of law at Ferrara University in 1920, a fascist deputy in 1924, Rector of Perugia University in 1925 and a professor (of the doctrine of the state) in 1927. Some syndicalists rapidly became efficient party managers and two of them, Cesare Rossi and Giovanni Marinelli, became close associates of Mussolini in 1919. Another, Michele Bianchi, became secretary of the party in 1921–22, the crucial period leading up to the March on Rome. Perhaps the best known syndicalist was the labour organiser Edmondo Rossoni, who led the fascist trade union confederation from 1922 to 1928. His aim was to establish a genuine autonomous syndical organisation and a corporative system in Italy. Mussolini had apparently supported these aims in the June programme of 1919 and the document was in fact written in part by yet another influential syndicalist, Alceste De Ambris, who then joined D'Annunzio in Fiume and drafted his *Carta del Carnaro*. De Ambris broke with Fascism when it began to protect bourgeois property and dropped many of its radical aims; he went into exile in France in 1923. Despite the disillusionment of many syndicalists, Rossoni attempted to convince Mussolini of the need to implement their programme. Increasingly suspicious of any autonomous movements and alarmed by Rossoni's growing reputation as the 'Duce of organised labour', Mussolini was reluctant to break with syndicalism completely. He did finally dismiss Rossoni in 1928, but he saw the importance of continuing to pay at least lip service to syndicalism; it gave his increasingly conservative regime a 'revolutionary' appearance which he hoped might satisfy left-wing fascists, and it also enabled him to curb the arrogance of the industrialists. *Confindustria*, the employers' organisation, needed to be counter-balanced by syndicalism.

Ex-socialists, *arditi*, republicans, Futurists and syndicalists all became 'Fascists of the first hour'. They had all been interventionists, had supported the war effort, had deplored Italy's betrayal by her allies at the peace settlement, and had all sought to sweep away an ineffective political system which seemed incapable of solving the country's post-war problems. Hostile towards the new mass parties of the Socialists and Catholics as well as the old liberal ruling elite, they had entered the elections of November 1919 and had been decisively repudiated. The movement had apparently been a failure and many of them deserted it. An alternative leader had emerged and had established a power base in the disputed seaport of Fiume. Not the least of Mussolini's problems by the end of 1919 was the appeal of Gabriele D'Annunzio to those very activists who had joined the Fascists after March 1919.

Notes

1 *Il Popolo d'Italia*, 24 March 1919. Reprinted in E. and D. Susmel (eds.), *Opera Omnia di Benito Mussolini*, Florence, 1953, xii, pp. 321–4.

2 A. Cassels, *Fascist Italy*, London, 1969, p. 15.

3 For this and other reminiscences see E. Ludwig, *Talks with Mussolini*, London, 1932.

4 C. Seton-Watson, *Italy from Liberalism to Fascism*, London, 1967, pp. 192–5.

5 Seton-Watson, *Italy*, p. 195.

6 P. Cannistraro (ed.), *Historical Dictionary of Fascist Italy*, Westport, 1982, pp. 198–200.

7 For the role of veterans in post-war Italy see G. Sabbatucci, *I Combattenti nel Primo Dopoguerra*, Bari, 1974.

8 M. Clark, *Modern Italy 1871–1982*, London, 1984, p. 214.

9 G. Bonfanti, *Il Fascismo, Brescia*, 1976, i, p. 32.

10 J. Joll, *Intellectuals in Politics*, London, 1960, p. 175.

11 A. Lyttelton, *The Seizure of Power*, London, 1973, p. 46.

2

Expansion and breakthrough, 1920–1922

The challenge of D'Annunzio

On 12 September 1919 D'Annunzio led a force of over a thousand volunteers and army deserters from Ronchi near Trieste to the disputed port of Fiume, which was still creating tension between Italy and her wartime allies. Rioting had broken out there in the summer, some French soldiers had been killed and the decision had been taken to reduce the size of the Italian contingent of the allied garrison in order to restore calm. This had infuriated local patriots and, most ominously, the military authorities in the area. Prime Minister Nitti was already under attack for his austerity programme, his acceleration of the demobilisation process and his granting of an amnesty to wartime deserters. D'Annunzio therefore readily accepted the invitation of some young officers to solve the Fiume question by direct action. He occupied the city and met with no resistance. He remained there until December 1920. So for well over a year he successfully defied his own government, the Yugoslavs in Belgrade and the allied powers. He also posed an acute problem for Mussolini and the fascist movement. If D'Annunzio succeeded and if his so-called 'legionaries' conquered not only Fiume but also Italy itself, fascism would cease to be relevant and Mussolini himself would, at best, become a mere lieutenant in the service of the Poet Hero. Disillusioned Italians could be expected to hail just one Man of Providence and not two – at least not simultaneously!

Born in Pescara on the Adriatic in 1863, D'Annunzio's earlier writings were already being published before Mussolini's birth and by the end of the century his erotic novels and scandalous

25

life-style made him notorious within Italy and beyond. Like Mussolini he was attracted by Friedrich Nietzsche's concept of the superman, and this was to add spice to their competition in the early 1920s. In 1897 he entered parliament and in 1900 amazed everyone by moving from the extreme right to the extreme left. It was the sort of theatrical gesture which he loved to make throughout his career. Very quickly he moved back to the right again and championed the cause of Italy's imperial greatness. His poetry extolling the virtues of a strong navy won him the support and lasting affection of nationalists, irredentists, navalists and all those who sought to revive memories of the Venetian empire in the Adriatic and eastern Mediterranean. In 1915 he became the most influential spokesman of the interventionist movement, before achieving even greater fame as a war hero because of his audacious feats, which included flying over Vienna to drop leaflets, a symbolic act which revealed the poet as propagandist, aviator and warrior. Perhaps these were the perfect credentials for superman status. The loss of an eye during these exploits and the appearance of a piratical eye-patch only enhanced his romantic appeal.

It was entirely appropriate for one of D'Annunzio's biographers to call him 'the first Duce'.[1] Very few Italians opposed his coup in Fiume and he did command widespread active support. Of crucial importance was the sympathetic attitude of the army. The recently redeemed borderlands of northeast Italy were still under military occupation and it was a unit garrisoning Ronchi which first called in D'Annunzio. Before long entire battalions deserted and ex-*arditi* and other veterans hastened to join these regulars. Army officers had a vested interest in D'Annunzio's success. Quite apart from their intense nationalism, they were keen to exaggerate the threat from the Slovenes and Croats because border tensions justified the retention of a large army and safeguarded their career prospects. The generals, however, tended to be more circumspect; indiscipline in the army was something they were reluctant to endorse and the involvement of the military in politics was a distinct departure from the traditional apolitical attitude adopted by the Italian army since 1861.[2] Nitti was, nevertheless, unwilling to test their loyalty so instead of ordering them to evict D'Annunzio he sent first General Badoglio and then General Caviglia to act as commissioners in Venezia Giulia to supervise the activities of troops in the border areas. Their instructions were to contain but not to provoke D'Annunzio and the rebels.

The coup in Fiume also won support from the navy, not only because D'Annunzio had written poems in praise of torpedo boats but because it was interested in acquiring bases along the Dalmatian coast. D'Annunzio could rely upon the even firmer backing of Giovanni Giulietti, the syndicalist leader of the seamen's union based in Genoa. He proved to be a staunch ally, always prepared to circumvent any proposed blockade of Fiume and to sanction acts of piracy. Another well-known syndicalist was, of course, De Ambris, who deserted Mussolini to act as D'Annunzio's chief economic adviser and became the author of the famous charter of September 1920, which proclaimed the establishment of a new political and economic order based on national syndicalism and corporativism. Fiume would become the model for the rest of Italy. De Ambris had many loyal supporters in the peninsula, especially around his stronghold of Parma; they were to prove this just over a year later when they fought long and hard against the Fascists who had first deserted D'Annunzio and then aligned themselves with reactionary landowners and industrialists.

Syndicalists were joined by other representatives from the ranks of the interventionists, including Nationalists, Futurists, irredentists and Fascists. D'Annunzio looked to Mussolini to organise support, act as his chief propagandist and collect funds. With most of patriotic Italy behind D'Annunzio, Mussolini could hardly refuse. He flew to Fiume on 7 October 1919 where he apparently urged caution, which enraged D'Annunzio and led to a series of acrimonious exchanges between the two men over the next fourteen months. In public Mussolini gave wholehearted support but in private he raised doubts and was soon being accused of diverting funds raised for Fiume into the coffers of the Fascist movement. When D'Annunzio announced his intention to march on Rome, Mussolini was unwilling to become his drummer boy and for two obvious reasons: by the spring of 1920 D'Annunzio's support was weakening – and even the people of Fiume were beginning to become disillusioned – and secondly, if anyone marched on Rome Mussolini had someone else in mind! The 'second Duce' certainly took careful note of the successes and failures of the 'first Duce'. The balcony speeches, the responses of the crowd, the blackshirts, the emphasis on nationalism and militarism, the promulgation of charters and the colourful rituals all became an integral part of fascist choreography. Perhaps Mussolini needed no guidance in these matters but it was useful to see them being rehearsed on the provincial stage of Fiume. There was no doubting D'Annunzio's charismatic qualities but he lacked steadiness of purpose and application. Above all, he was too self-consciously the poet and the intellectual instead of being the ruthless, opportunistic and astute political leader. Ironically, his seizure of Fiume, which won such initial acclaim, and his decision to establish there his so-called Regency were his biggest mistakes. By placing himself on the frontier, by failing to advance, he became isolated and marginalised. If the struggle to occupy political space is one of the themes of post-war Italy then D'Annunzio miscalculated. It was the streets and squares of Italy ('piazza politics') and not the territory of Fiume which had to be conquered and occupied. Mussolini saw this quite clearly. His socialist opponents – like D'Annunzio – did not. They occupied factories in the cities and fields in the countryside and they also won control of municipal councils and exercised power through their cooperatives, trade unions and *camere del lavoro* (chambers of labour), but because they failed to take command of the streets they were defeated by formidable adversaries who did.

Squadrismo: the Fascist offensive

It will be seen how on at least three occasions Prime Minister Giolitti unwittingly assisted the fascist movement. One such occasion was the decision to expel D'Annunzio from Fiume by forceful military action in December 1920. The legionaries retreated and dispersed, many of them joining or rejoining Mussolini's *fasci*. This increased the number of militant activists in an already expanding fascist organisation. The defeat of D'Annunzio was a fatal blow to his prestige. For Mussolini it was the virtual elimination of a dangerous rival. It is interesting to note that he had accepted the Treaty of Rapallo which foreign minister Carlo Sforza had signed with the Yugoslavs in the previous month, a settlement which created free city status for

Fiume.

Another of Giolitti's decisions was to continue with a policy of state neutrality in labour relations, which dated back to the general strike of 1904. The years 1919–20 became known as the *biennio rosso* (two years dominated by the red revolutionary threat), and the wave of strikes which swept Italian cities culminated in the 'occupation of the factories' during August and September 1920. Most affected were Milan and Turin where sit-ins took place as the workers' response to the growing intransigence of the owners, who were rapidly recovering their nerve and had formed the *Confindustria* (confederation of industrialists) in March 1920. Resentful of the economic demands of the workers and their call for the recognition of factory councils being put forward by left-wing socialists like Antonio Gramsci, the owners sought assistance from the government. They were convinced that a revolution was in progress and that a Soviet regime would be installed unless the authorities reacted. Giolitti was perceptive enough to realise that the occupation of the factories was not the beginning of a revolution but the climax of a strike movement. He calculated that calling in the police and the army to evict the workers was unnecessary and likely to be counter-productive. Giolitti put pressure on the employers to make concessions, a compromise was worked out and the workers evacuated the factories. As he had predicted, the strike movement began to wane and organised labour began a long retreat. What he failed to realise was that the industrialists felt that they had been humiliated and were determined to revenge themselves, that they had lost confidence in the willingness or ability of the state to protect them and that they might look elsewhere for this protection. Mussolini was faced with yet another of his many dilemmas. To mobilise his action squads (*squadre d'azione*) to defend the property of these frightened industrialists would lay him open to the charge of allowing his *squadristi* to become the tools of capitalism. It would mean abandoning even more of his original, radical programme; in addition, he ran the risk of losing those 'fascists of the first hour' who joined the squads to spearhead a coup, not to become the bodyguards of the old conservative order. But all this was happening anyway. Mussolini personally had long been in receipt of funds from the Perrone brothers of Ansaldo (the huge industrial cartel of northern Italy), and his blackshirts were increasingly called upon to act as strike-breakers and security guards by frightened businessmen and bankers. Mussolini had already lost Marinetti, Vecchi and De Ambris as a result of his more conservative policies and his ambiguous attitude towards D'Annunzio. He could afford to dispense with these left-wingers because their places were being filled by an influx of young, lower middle-class recruits from the universities, the civil service and 'respectable' bourgeois families. Like Giolitti, Mussolini saw the occupation of the factories as a turning point, clear evidence that revolution was not on the agenda of the leading socialists and trade unionists. He could now intensify the anti-socialism of the movement, conceal his belief that the red menace was receding and claim that his assault on the strongholds of the left would free the workers from their Marxist overlords. In return for money, arms and transport for his expanding movement, in the knowledge that the state authorities would be inclined to help rather than hinder his activities, Mussolini was more than prepared to unleash the *squadristi* against the common enemies of both fascism and capitalism. Their effectiveness had been dramatically revealed in incidents like the burning of the Balkan Hotel in Trieste on 13 July 1920 and the routing of the Slovene socialists and their Italian comrades on the left.

Similar developments were also taking place in the countryside, particularly in the Po valley and Tuscany. These were areas where Socialist and Populist leagues, co-operatives and trade unions had established a firm hold. Victories in the local elections of November 1920 gave Socialists and Populists control over an impressive number of municipal councils. They dominated the *camere del lavoro*, fixed wage rates and ran the employment agencies. The landowners and many tenant farmers, local shopkeepers and artisans bitterly resented being subjected to this left-wing authoritarianism. What particularly alarmed the landowners was the unauthorised occupation of private land, often directed by the local cooperatives and councils. Most ominous of all was the knowledge that these illegalities were being condoned by the governments of Nitti and Giolitti. The prefects, the police and the army were obliged to remain aloof. After all, the wartime governments had promised 'land to the peasants'. This was the situation which prompted the rise of what has been called 'rural fascism'. Like the northern industrialists, the landowners looked around for the assistance denied them by the state. Their sons and those of other local dignitaries were prepared to react and many of them had served as officers but they were too few and too scattered to confront the leagues without outside support. The wealth of the gentry had to be used to purchase this support from the larger towns where squads could be organised, armed and provided with lorries. Sometimes they wore the blueshirts of the Nationalists, sometimes they were mafia-type criminals, the unemployed and the unemployable (a strange mixture of 'gentlemen' and ruffians not uncommon in the Renaissance, the Risorgimento and the Resistance), but usually they were blackshirts attached to the rapidly growing number of *fasci*. The latter were commanded by new leaders or *ras* as they came to be called (*ras* was the name given to Ethiopian chiefs). By the end of 1920 there were 88 *fasci* with over 20,000 members; by the end of 1921 there were 834 with almost 250,000, an increase largely attributable to agrarian fascism.[3] Local initiatives accounted for much of these activities but Mussolini in Milan, although initially amazed and suspicious of such spontaneity, strove to maintain control and some semblance of discipline. The need to assert his authority over the *ras* became most pressing in the spring of 1921 because Mussolini saw an opportunity for entering national politics and perhaps securing power by legal, parliamentary means. This was not a manoeuvre welcomed by the swashbuckling provincial leaders of agrarian fascism.

Giolitti's third error of judgement was his decision to call for elections in May 1921 in an attempt to secure a more amenable chamber of deputies. The Fascists were invited to join his National Bloc. The offer was accepted and 35 Fascists, including their leader, won seats. But despite the widespread violence – and there were 40 deaths on polling day alone – the PPI increased its representation and the Socialists still managed to elect 123 deputies, despite victimisation and the competition from their former comrades in the newly created Communist Party, which won 15 seats. The chamber remained unmanageable so Giolitti resigned, never to return. In his maiden speech in Parliament on 21 June, Mussolini showed his contempt for the democratic system, for Giolitti's attempts to win Fascist support, and for all left-wing parties, but he did indicate a willingness to abandon

31

violence if others did so. He asserted that Fascism was not anti-clerical and believed that an accommodation with the Vatican was possible; nor was fascism hostile to social legislation or to the trade union leaders of the CGL. Still less – was Fascism opposed to capitalism or concepts of economic liberalism.[4] These were correctly interpreted as signals that Mussolini was seriously considering an alternative route to power through legal and parliamentary channels. This was good news for liberals who hoped that Fascist leaders might become 'respectable' and, if allowed government posts, more responsible. But it was bad news for *ras* like Italo Balbo in Ferrara and Dino Grandi in Bologna, who advocated the direct route to power through the continuation of the military operations of the *squadristi*. From this point onwards there was tension within the Fascist movement between those pressing for a political solution and those supporting the military approach. This was a serious threat to the cohesion of the movement and to Mussolini's leadership. The first trial of strength came in the summer of 1921.

On 2 August 1921 Mussolini agreed to the signing of a Pact of Pacification to bring about a truce in the rapidly escalating civil war. He did this for several reasons. Beginning to relish his role as a parliamentarian he realised that the violence of the squads was alienating middle-class opinion. Large columns of *squadristi*, well armed and transported in lorries, were converging on villages and towns, burning down the headquarters of Socialist and Catholic organisations, beating opponents with clubs (the 'sacred *manganello*') and forcing them to drink castor oil. This reign of terror was succeeding in 'converting' whole areas, which had been strongholds of socialism, to support for fascism (see Documents 6 and 7). It was also bringing the threat of anarchy and retaliation. Left-wing activists, for example, were organising *arditi del popolo* to resist the blackshirts and at Sarzana on 31 July twelve *carabinieri* had routed five hundred fascists, a warning to Mussolini and the *ras* of what might happen elsewhere if the new Prime Minister Bonomi decided to enforce law and order with greater severity. To Mussolini it seemed an opportune moment for a truce. The *ras* rejected it, convinced that agrarian fascism would lose impetus just as it was on the point of liquidating its enemies. Mussolini was infuriated by this indiscipline. 'Fascism can do without me?' he asked. 'Doubtless, but I too can do very well without fascism.'[5] On 17 August he resigned from the national executive. Balbo and the other provincial leaders remained unimpressed. They could, and on occasions did, turn to D'Annunzio as a more dynamic Duce, but they were convinced that they could induce Mussolini to change his mind. After all, they were the *veri fascisti* (the true fascists), the spearhead of the fascist revolution. Balbo, born in Ferrara in 1896, an interventionist in 1914, a lieutenant in the *Alpini* during the war, a university student at Florence in 1918, a member of the Ferrara *fascio* in January 1921 and its secretary the following month, was obviously a supremely self-confident young man with a distaste for standing still. He was also a competent organiser and within a few months emerged as the most charismatic and daring of all the *squadristi*. He and Grandi rejected any idea of a truce and their defiance of Mussolini in September was calculated and magnificent. With several thousand *squadristi* they 'occupied' Ravenna on the anniversary of D'Annunzio's coup in Fiume and paid homage at the grave of Dante. Apart from these symbolic gestures they proved that they were the masters of central Italy. Mussolini responded by revealing that when it came to political tactics he was the master.

A compromise was arranged at the Rome congress of the Fascists in November 1921. Mussolini acknowledged *squadrismo* as an indispensable and integral part of the movement and the *ras* recognised him as the indispensable Duce. The movement was converted into a political party, the National Fascist Party (PNF), so that Mussolini could exert more control and perform his political duties as a party leader. There was a public reconciliation with Grandi and the *ras* accepted the more conservative line adopted at the congress. In return, Mussolini repudiated the truce with the Socialists. National syndicalism was discussed as Fascist unions were being constructed in many areas and the Duce's insistence that they be brought under party control was reluctantly accepted. Rossoni, who established the General Confederation of Syndical Corporations in January 1922, tried unsuccessfully over many years to achieve greater autonomy for the labour movement. As the new party appeared to have discarded most of its radical demands, funds flowed in from both the industrial and agrarian sectors. This enabled party secretary Bianchi to improve the efficiency of its political organisation and the effectiveness of its military wing, increasingly referred to as the party militia. But Bianchi and Mussolini were keen to underline the unique character of the PNF, which was 'a party which is also a militia'. This greater unity enabled the party to bid for power just as its political rivals – the Liberals, the Socialists and Catholics – were rapidly falling apart.

The March on Rome

The collapse of the Bonomi government in February 1922, followed by the two inglorious ministries of Luigi Facta, vividly illustrated the political disarray of liberal Italy. Facta only agreed to serve on the understanding that he would soon be replaced by his patron Giolitti. The liberals themselves were divided into at least four factions, some in favour of an anti-fascist front but most inclined towards appeasement. Ex-premiers Salandra, Orlando, Nitti and Giolitti all believed in the possibility of an accommodation with Mussolini and he cleverly kept them hoping and guessing for the next nine months. The Populists were similarly disunited, with a right wing of moderates and conservatives who deplored confrontation with Fascism, and a left wing whose activists were bearing the brunt of attacks by the *squadristi*, especially in the area around Cremona where the local *ras* Roberto Farinacci was acquiring notoriety. The election of the new pope Pius XI was a severe blow for democratic Catholics and for the secretary of the PPI, Luigi Sturzo. Pius XI's experiences as nuncio in Poland after the war had reinforced his anti-Bolshevism and as archbishop of Milan he had blessed the banners of the Fascists. He was not prepared to support Sturzo or the left wing of his party, and the Vatican sought to dissociate itself from the Populists and to obstruct attempts at an anti-fascist coalition. The Socialists, even after the departure of the Communists, were in worse shape than the liberals and Catholics. Serrati's maximalist rhetoric from the centre of the party was ridiculed by the extremists on the left and Filippo Turati's reformists on the right. Only when it was too little too late did Turati agree to join with democrats and Catholics to safeguard constitutional liberties, and nothing came of the manoeuvre. At least the Socialist trade union, (CGT), combined with others to form the Labour Alliance in February 1922 but it was boycotted by Catholics, Communists and, of course, Fascists. Its call for a general strike against Fascism in August proved a total disaster.

This 'parliamentary paralysis', as Gaetano Salvemini called it, together with serious divisions within the labour movement, gave Mussolini an excellent opportunity to make a significant political breakthrough.[6] Assured of regular financial contributions from industrialists as well as landowners, he and other members of the National Council of the party could now afford to widen the scope of their journalistic and propaganda activities and improve the efficiency of their organisation. This was vitally important for two reasons. The dramatic increase in the size of the party was a threat to its coherence and this required urgent measures to enforce discipline; secondly, the equally dramatic increase in the size of the areas which were under fascist control demanded the presence of party activists and administrators to consolidate these gains. In speeches designed to reassure the wealthy middle classes, Mussolini presented the acceptable face of fascism – a movement and now a party pledged to restore Italian power and prestige, to revive the economy by increasing productivity and abolishing harmful state controls, and to re-establish law and order by curbing left-wing subversives. This last claim was outrageously cynical in view of the escalating violence of the *squadristi*. Mussolini realised this but to disown the *ras* would destroy the compromise of the Rome congress, endanger the unity of the party and bring to a halt the spectacular expansion of fascism in northern and central Italy. On the other hand, Mussolini was uncomfortably aware that the 'columns of fire' and brutalities of men like Farinacci, Balbo and Grandi could produce a backlash. Indeed, one of his constant preoccupations throughout 1922 and beyond was the possibility of an anti-Fascist front. If pushed too far Socialists, Catholics and liberals might forge a popular alliance and look to the king, D'Annunzio or Salandra for leadership, and if they won the support of the army and state officials Fascism would face extinction. This accounts for Mussolini's caution in the summer of 1922 and his persistent attempts to maintain some sort of political dialogue with Salandra, Orlando and even Giolitti. It was only when these efforts seemed to be failing, when an anti-Fascist combination became a distinct possibility, that he swept caution aside and launched his March on Rome. It has been acutely observed that 'the March on Rome was planned not because parliamentary paralysis had become intolerable, but because parliamentary paralysis might come to an end in a coalition of democratic groups'.[7] It was a decision which created alarm among the moderates of the party, but it was greeted with relief and enthusiasm by militant *ras* like Balbo.[8]

Since the beginning of the year dissidents within the party, like the ex-syndicalist Piero Marsich, had been pressing Mussolini to adopt the military solution, threatening to approach D'Annunzio again if he rejected their advice. By April he had successfully marginalised them but was virtually powerless when he attempted the same tactics against prestigious leaders like Grandi and Balbo. They were determined to resume their paramilitary operations and this time they were intent upon going further than the terrorisation of Socialist and Catholic leagues; they aimed to challenge the state itself. In May 1922, for instance, when Balbo occupied Ferrara he acted as the spokesman for the 50,000 unemployed he had brought with him and refused to evacuate the city until the government had agreed to finance an ambitious scheme for public works (see Document 3). Two weeks later it was the turn of Bologna, and there the fascist demand was for the removal of an unfriendly prefect. Again, the government of Facta gave way; again, the liberal state proved unwilling or unable to assert its authority. In July Farinacci wreaked such destruction in Cremona that it almost produced the backlash which Mussolini most feared. In the same month Rimini and Ravenna were occupied and these incidents did at last provoke a response. While the politicians dithered, the Labour Alliance called a general strike on 31 July. It played straight into the hands of the Fascists. It was poorly supported and the Fascists warned Facta that if the government refused to take action they certainly would. As 'the party of law and order' armed blackshirts ran essential services and won the praise of the middle classes; it was the Fascists and not the government who were prepared to protect them from the Bolshevik menace. On 3 August the strike was called off. In a famous phrase Turati called this the Caporetto of the workers (Caporetto was the traumatic defeat of the Italian army in October 1917). After this fiasco the socialist movement rapidly disintegrated. The *ras* took advantage of this and Ancona, Livorno, Genoa and Milan were occupied. In October the Fascists took over Trent and Bolzano, forcing the authorities to take stern measures against the Germans in the South Tyrol and any 'Austrian sympathisers' in the Trentino. By October 1922 only Turin and Parma had offered serious resistance. Apart from Apulia, the south of Italy had largely escaped the violence of the *squadristi*. So had Rome, and this was the greatest prize of all.

Throughout the summer of 1922 Mussolini had performed two roles. As the Duce of Fascism and the editor of *Il Popolo d'Italia* he had jubilantly recorded the 'victories' of the blackshirts. As the leader of the PNF he had negotiated with all the key political figures, impressing upon them his willingness to restore stability by ending the civil strife and his firm intention to seek political power through legal channels. He was shrewd enough to realise that the extra-parliamentary successes were largely illusory, that the momentum could easily be lost and that decisive action by the government, the police and the army could rapidly demoralise and destroy the movement. This was why he made his speech at Udine on 20 September, reassuring the king, the monarchists and the army officers that they had nothing to fear provided they did nothing to obstruct his patriotic followers (see Document 3). It was also why he took very seriously the possibility of Giolitti's return – the memory of the Fiume episode was still fresh in everyone's mind. Prime Minister Facta was not only the loyal lieutenant of Giolitti, he was also the personal friend of D'Annunzio and there was a scheme afoot to reconcile these two old adversaries. The Poet would speak to a rally of veterans at the Capitol on armistice day, 4 November, call for unity and prepare the ground for a new coalition government led by Giolitti, which would include Fascists if they chose to join it. Mussolini decided to sabotage this plan. On 16 October he signed a pact with D'Annunzio and Giulietti in which he agreed to disband the Fascist union at Genoa and allow Giulietti's seamen's union to represent the sailors in negotiations with the shipowners. In return for this concession, D'Annunzio agreed to demobilise his legionaries. On 25 October he cancelled his speech for the rally on 4 November. During this same period Mussolini finalised his plans for the March on Rome. Four quadrumvirs were appointed – Balbo, Bianchi, Cesare De Vecchi and General De Bono – the three commanders of the fascist militia chosen the previous August together with Bianchi, the secretary general of the party.

Only Bianchi and Balbo were keen to take action, the other two counselling delay. They argued that the squads were unprepared and De Vecchi, a convinced monarchist, hoped for a parliamentary solution with the Duce taking office in a national government led by Salandra. They were, however, outvoted and the planned insurrection went ahead.

When Mussolini had been asked whether the Fascists would join a new coalition government he had replied that no decision could be taken until after the meeting of the Fascist congress at Naples on 24 October. This duly took place and as thousands of blackshirts converged on the city the tension rose. Facta had already ordered General Pugliese to reinforce the garrison and defend Rome in case the squads attempted to enter the capital on their way to or from Naples. At the congress the Duce made a speech calling on Facta to admit fascists to key posts in the cabinet or face insurrection. There was a parade in the evening and the following day the congress ended and the leaders and delegates dispersed. Mussolini returned to Milan to continue his contacts with Giolitti, Nitti and Salandra. Balbo went to Perugia, which had been designated the command centre for the quadrumvirs who would co-ordinate the March on Rome. Grandi, De Vecchi and Costanzo Ciano left for Rome to be available to negotiate with government circles. When it became clear that the fascist mobilisation was not apparently taking place immediately, Facta relaxed. He had, however, completely misread the situation and on 26 October Salandra, De Vecchi and others urged him to resign. They insisted that failure to comply would force the Fascists to launch their planned insurrection. The cabinet was split over this issue and gave Facta a free hand to decide upon his next move. He obviously preferred a Giolitti/Mussolini coalition to one led by Salandra but failed to convince his patron that his presence was urgently required in Rome. The king, however, did respond to the crisis and arrived in the capital the following day, apparently prepared to keep Facta in office and to take a firm stand against Fascist threats. There was no time to be lost because that very evening the *ras* began the occupation of many cities in northern and central Italy. The prefects, the police and the army were uncertain how to react.

At 5 a.m. on 28 October the cabinet, convinced they had royal support, agreed to proclaim a state of siege. Martial law would enable the army and the police to dispose of the Fascist threat and General Pugliese, with 25,000 troops and the backing of National-ist blueshirts, would easily crush any Fascist columns which attempted to advance on Rome. At 9 a.m. Facta went to secure the king's signature. He was shattered to learn that Victor Emmanuel had changed his mind and refused to sign, a decision which was made public two hours later. There have been many attempts to explain the king's action. Diaz and other leading generals are supposed to have indicated that 'the army will do its duty but it would be better not to put it to the test'; rumours of a 'plot' to replace the king with his pro-fascist first cousin the Duke of Aosta are believed to have influenced his decision, and northern industrialists like Silvio Crespi and Antonio Benni voiced their opposition to a confrontation with Fascism. These are all valid explanations. The king was not a forceful character but he was quite shrewd and must have realised rapidly that there was no consensus in favour of a show-down with Mussolini. All the leading politicians favoured accommodation and that included Facta himself; the generals, the prefects, indus-trial magnates and landowners, newspaper editors, like Luigi Albertini, and the church all had grave reservations about any move which might create even more disorder and destruction, leaving Italy at the mercy of the subversives of the left. To pre-serve his throne and to prevent civil war, the king backed down, accepted Facta's resignation and asked Salandra to form a new government.

Salandra realised that a successful coalition would have to include Fascists. He offered them four cabinet posts. De Vecchi, Ciano and Grandi urged Mussolini to accept but he now sensed that he was master of the situation and rejected the offer. Salandra announced his failure to the king and intimated that Mussolini would have to be summoned. When it was absolutely clear that he was being asked to form a new government, Mussolini left Milan in the evening of 29 October. He met the king the following day, bringing with him he said the Italy of Vittorio Veneto (the final victory of Italy over the Austrians in 1918). On 31 October he announced his cabinet and on the same day 70,000 blackshirts marched through Rome to be saluted by the king, General Diaz and Admiral Thaon di Revel. They then moved on to greet their leader, the new prime minister of Italy. They had arrived the previous day by various modes of transport *after* the legal transfer of power. There had not in fact been a March on Rome, only the threat of one. It had not been Mussolini's intention to execute a *military* coup in Rome but to convince as many people as possible that the seizure of strategic points in so many northern cities could be repeated in the capital. This bluff succeeded, enabling Mussolini to carry out a *political* coup. Unwittingly, Balbo and the blackshirts provided the illusion of Fascist invincibility which proved sufficient to secure for Mussolini the premiership. For some this was the 'Fascist revolution'; for others this was just another coalition government emerging from the tumult and confusion of extraordinary events. For Mussolini it was the reality of power that mattered. With its combination of illusion and reality the March on Rome was a fitting prelude to the fascist regime which was created four years later.

Notes

1 M. Ledeen, *The First Duce*, Baltimore, 1977. See also R. De Felice, *D'Annunzio politico*, Bari, 1978.

2   This is the major theme of J. Whittam, *The Politics of the Italian Army*, London, 1977.

3 R. De Felice, *Mussolini il fascista*, Turin, 1966, ii, p. 5.

4 C. Delzell (ed.), *Mediterranean Fascism 1919–45*, New York, 1970, pp. 22–5.

5 C. Seton-Watson, *Italy from Liberalism to Fascism*, London, 1967, p. 594.

6 G. Salvemini, *The Origins of Fascism*, New York, 1973, p. 368. This was written in 1942.

7 Salvemini, *Origins*, p. 368.

8 C. Balbo, *Diario 1922*, Milan, 1932, p. 179.

3

Transition: from coalition to regime, 1922–1928

A government which governs

From the beginning the true significance of the March on Rome was in dispute. For radical blackshirts it was quite simply the Fascist Revolution – a view endorsed by party propagandists – and they eagerly anticipated a New Order which would dispense with the old ruling class and sweep away the ideas and institutions associated with liberal Italy. For moderates in the party and their non-Fascist sympathisers it was more of a Restoration, the reassertion of authoritarian government as a prerequisite for what they called 'normalisation'. Far from being swept away, the monarchy, the army, the bureaucracy, the productive middle classes and even the church would all play key roles in strengthening state power. Those illegalities which had so disrupted national life – perpetrated both by subversives of the left and by the *squadristi* – would no longer be tolerated. Tension between radicals and moderates persisted throughout the Fascist period and Mussolini shrewdly realised that this could be manipulated to his own advantage. He wished to combine at least the illusion of revolutionary dynamism with the reality of political power. With activists competing with more conservative elements within the PNF, the Duce could act as mediator, divide and rule and keep everyone guessing. He could also rely on the support of both in his avowed aim of constructing a government which governed. 'Our programme is simple', he had announced at Udine on 20 September, 'we want to govern Italy' (see Document 3).

Mussolini's first cabinet disappointed his more ardent follow-

41

ers but reassured the moderates. It was a coalition government consisting of four fascists, four assorted liberals, two Populists and one Nationalist. General Diaz and Admiral Thaon di Revel took over the ministries of the armed services and the philosopher Giovanni Gentile became minister of public instruction and the leading ideologue of Fascism for the next decade (he joined the PNF in June 1923). Mussolini himself was not only prime minister but also interior minister and foreign minister. He placed one of the quadrumvirs, De Bono, in charge of the police. Even so, it looked a safe and respectable team with advocates of both continuity and change fairly evenly balanced. Clearly it was premature to speak of a 'Fascist Italy', although Mussolini's first speech to parliament as premier on 16 November warned the deputies that with 300,000 armed blackshirts behind him he could have constructed an exclusively Fascist administration and converted their building into a barracks. 'I could have done', he concluded, 'but at least for the present I do not wish to do so'.[1] The message was clear. If deputies and senators supported his measures there would be no need for any sudden, violent transformation of state and society. The message was received and understood. Both chambers gave the new government votes of confidence together with plenary powers to reform the fiscal and administrative systems.

The law to streamline and decentralise the administrative system and to make economies by amalgamating various ministries was hardly the dynamic start which most Fascists expected. The purge of some anti-Fascist personnel was welcome but the reforms were poorly co-ordinated and by 1926 were generally regarded as having failed.[2] The appointment of Mussolini had led his followers to believe that lucrative posts awaited them and that they would displace the old ruling elites. For three years veterans and blackshirts had anticipated their entry into the promised land. Many of them became angry and frustrated – and by July 1923 party membership had risen to 800,000 – when they failed to receive their just rewards. It became so difficult to maintain discipline within the party that Dino Grandi, rapidly distancing himself from the unruly *squadrismo* of the past two years, actually advocated its abolition![3] This was not so bizarre, as Mussolini himself had written in August 1921: 'For me fascism is not an end in itself. It was a means to re-establish national equilibrium'.[4] In the second sentence he is prepared to use the past tense! After the March on Rome, however, dissolving the PNF was not a serious option. Without the party and the 300,000 armed men mentioned in his speech of 16 November Mussolini was unlikely to remain prime minister for very long. He held that post *because* he was the Duce of Fascism. Acting as head of government in the 'king's Italy' and party leader in 'Fascist Italy' were exacting tasks. It was a kind of diarchy, only with one man playing both roles. There were even separate anthems, the *Marcia reale* for royalist and conservative Italy and *Giovinezza* (sung by the *arditi* in the war) for Fascist Italy. To be secure Mussolini had to consolidate his power in both sectors.

Delighted with the administrative and economic reforms of the new government, moderates and liberals accepted the need for stern measures against disturbers of the peace *provided* they were implemented through legal channels. As prime minister, Mussolini supported this 'normalisation'; as Duce he reserved the right to proceed against his enemies and critics by other means. This involved the creation of a secret 'cheka' (named after Lenin's ruthless organisation for the defence of the Bolshevik revolution), a group of criminal hit men whose task was the terrorisation of dissenters inside and outside the party. Led by Amerigo Dumini, who was allocated an office in the Palazzo Viminale, the ministry of the interior, they were controlled by some of the Duce's closest advisers, Aldo Finzi (under-secretary of the interior under the minister, who was, of course, Mussolini himself), Cesare Rossi (head of the Duce's press office) and Giovanni Marinelli (administrative secretary and fund raiser for the PNF). These men were at the very centre of the new power structure and achieved notoriety in 1924 when they were all implicated in the Matteotti murder which almost toppled Mussolini. It was the continuation of such illegalities which increasingly alarmed liberals like Luigi Albertini, the editor of the *Corriere della sera*, and elder statesmen like Salandra, Orlando and Giolitti.

Unlike the clandestine cheka, the Fascist Grand Council which was established on 15 December 1922 and met for the first time the following month, was publicly acknowledged to be the supreme organ of the fascist party. It was a consultative body totally dominated by Mussolini, a kind of alternative cabinet which included all the leading Fascists. Although it took many fundamental decisions it only acquired legal status in 1928. Mussolini used it to reinforce his authority within the PNF, to establish a clear hierarchy and to keep possible rivals under close observation. Ironically, it provided the setting for the Duce's fall from power in July 1943 (see Document 17). One of its first acts was the transformation of the *squadre* into a national militia (*Milizia volontaria per la sicurezza nazionale*: MVSN). De Bono was placed in command of 300,000 blackshirts, who swore allegiance not to the king but to the Duce. It was another attempt by Mussolini to discipline his unruly followers and to balance party and state institutions, his own private army against the regular army. It perhaps created as many problems as it solved. It took at least four years for the *ras* to come to heel, it irritated the king and alarmed the army, who took advantage of the Matteotti crisis to reassert their authority.

By pursuing legal and extra-legal methods – often hopelessly entangled – the new government harassed its left-wing critics. Mussolini had tried to reach an accommodation with the leaders of the CGL (the Socialist general confederation of labour) but this was bitterly opposed by the *ras* and had to be abandoned. Socialists, Communists, Populists and even D'Annunzio's legionaries were put under constant pressure. Nor were freemasons exempt, despite the fact that so many fascist leaders had become members (Balbo, Farinacci, Costanzo Ciano, Rossoni, De Bono, Acerbo and Rossi). Mussolini declared war on all secret societies and in February 1923 freemasonry and Fascism were declared incompatible, a decision which at least pleased the church. In June 1924 it was the turn of the mafia when Cesare Mori was sent to Sicily to destroy it.[5] He had some success but, most important for Mussolini, the campaign provided the newspapers with exciting headlines which enhanced the prestige of the regime. Always acutely conscious of the influence of newspapers, Mussolini secured decree powers in July 1923 to curb the press. He chose not to implement them immediately but held them in reserve and was able to activate them a year later during the Matteotti affair.

In this piecemeal fashion the new government sought to construct an authoritarian state. Despite the rhetoric, the role of the PNF was as yet unclear and the position of parliament uncertain.

The situation remained fluid and it was difficult to discern whether a cautious conservatism would prevail over the more outrageous *me ne frego* ('I dont give a damn' – the slogan of *arditi* and legionaries adopted by the blackshirts) tendencies of Fascist activists. The former approach was reinforced by the fusion of the Nationalists with the PNF in February 1923.

The entry of the Nationalists

All Fascists, whatever their provenance, were nationalists, as the name of their party indicated. Since 1910, however, there had been a small but very influential group of Italians calling themselves Nationalists. The Italian Nationalist Association (ANI) had been founded by Enrico Corradini and Luigi Federzoni. Corradini's ideas had attracted the attention of syndicalists and some socialists like Mussolini (see Document 5). The concept of Italy as a 'proletarian nation' where national competition was substituted for class conflict gained widespread interest. The Nationalists did not seek to build up a mass following, however, but were unashamedly elitist and relied upon their close links with big business, the officer corps, and other powerful pressure groups among imperialists, irredentists and intellectuals in order to promote their ideas. *Idea nazionale* was their newspaper, advocating a vigorous colonial policy, high tariffs, state control of unions and a strong executive. Alfredo Rocco developed many of these ideas before and after the First World War. The Nationalists had played a significant part in bringing about both the Libyan war and Italy's entry into the European war in 1915. Consistently anti-socialist and hostile towards Giolitti and the liberal state, they sought to impose their expansionist doctrines and their call for a strong, authoritarian state upon the veterans' associations which sprang up after the war and later upon the Fascists themselves. With close ties to the court, the army, the agrarians and industrialists, they attempted to remain independent. Although they often co-operated with Fascists they maintained their own private army of blueshirts, and conflict with the blackshirts was not a rare occurrence. They were, for instance, prepared to help General Pugliese in the defence of Rome in October 1922 and over the following weeks repeatedly clashed with local *ras* in the south of Italy. But the similarity of aims between the ANI and the PNF proved to be stronger than their differences. Federzoni joined Mussolini's government as colonial minister, although he would have preferred to serve under Salandra and to have been appointed foreign minister. Reluctantly adjusting to the new situation, Federzoni and his fellow Nationalists concluded that their policies were more likely to be implemented if they joined the PNF. After protracted negotiations a Pact of Union was signed in February 1923 and the formal fusion of the two parties was concluded at a meeting with Mussolini at the Palazzo Chigi on 7 March. The ten Nationalist deputies increased the number of fascists in parliament to forty (in a chamber of 535!) and their 80,000 blueshirts of the *Sempre Pronti!* joined the militia – much to the disgust of the provincial *ras*. But the Nationalists had always believed more in quality than in quantity and this was the true significance of the fusion.[6]

Mussolini had once described the PNF as a party of facts and not theories. With Giovanni Gentile as a ministerial colleague and with the influx of Nationalists into the party this description would soon require modification. Men like Rocco, Corradini and Roberto Forges Davanzati were brimming with ideas and were determined to put them into practice. They have been called 'reactionary Fabians' because by permeating the Fascist party they aimed to transform the state. With their emphasis on discipline, professionalism and elitism, they felt well qualified to present a clearly defined blueprint for the design of an authoritarian state. 'A place for everything and everything in its place' would express their views in colloquial fashion or even – in Mussolini's famous slogan – 'Everything in the state, nothing against the state, nothing outside the state'. Their real opportunity arose during the Matteotti crisis when Federzoni and Rocco were given the responsibility for constructing a firm basis for the Fascist regime. Despite their efforts they never really succeeded. The chaotic nature of Fascism itself and Mussolini's style of government proved to be intractable obstacles. Giuseppe Bottai, a 'revisionist Fascist' who shared many of the managerial and technocratic views of the Nationalists, had written that in 1922 'the fascisms marched on Rome . . . In Rome we have to found fascism'.[7] There were always too many varieties of Fascism for this aim to be fulfilled.

The Matteotti crisis

Even with the addition of the ex-Nationalists the Fascist representation in parliament was still ludicrously small. Mussolini had three alternatives. He could abolish parliament, which would seem logical for a movement which claimed to be anti-parliamentarian and revolutionary; it would also be welcomed by radical Fascists. He could change the rules, dissolve the chamber and win a safe majority in the next elections; this would satisfy the moderates and liberals. Finally, he could continue with the existing system, constantly searching for support among the parties to win majorities for his coalition government. Apart from the obvious inconvenience, the last option depended largely on the votes of the Populists and in April 1923 he decided to 'accept the resignation' of the PPI ministers. Mussolini had already met secretly with Cardinal Gasparri in January to discuss the possibility of resolving the Roman question. They agreed to postpone the issue and it was clear that both men regarded the PPI as an obstacle in the path of better church-state relations.[8] Pressure was soon exerted on the secretary of the party, the priest Luigi Sturzo; he resigned in June and was virtually forced into exile by the Vatican the following year. Uncertainty over the attitude of the Populists eliminated the third option and, as Mussolini was unready to dispense with parliament, he decided upon electoral reform.

The fascist deputy Giacomo Acerbo introduced a bill which would enable the party winning most seats, providing it secured at least 25 per cent of votes cast, to be entitled to two-thirds of the seats in the chamber. After bitter debates and fascist threats the bill was approved by the chamber in July and the senate in November. The Acerbo law had been opposed only by Socialists and Communists, the PPI having abstained. Liberals and democrats voted for it because they realised that if it was defeated parliament would be abolished; they also believed that it would bring an end to the chronic political instability which had plagued liberal Italy. The irony was that the Acerbo law proved to be unnecessary.

Parliament was dissolved in January 1924 and new elections were held on 6 April against a background of systematic terror and illegality. Mussolini's chosen candidates won 66 per cent of the votes and secured 374 deputies. More surprising was the fact that two and a half million were brave enough to vote for the opposition. They returned 39 PPI deputies, 19 Communists, 22 Socialists (PSI) and 24 reformist Socialists (PSU). Giacomo Matteotti, the leader of the PSU, rose in the new parliament on 30 May to denounce fascist violence and to deny the validity of the April elections. This infuriated Mussolini, who made no secret of his displeasure. On 10 June, on his way to parliament, Matteotti was attacked and bundled into a car. This was the work of Dumini and the cheka but there were witnesses to the kidnapping, the ownership of the car was discovered and this led the investigation to Rossi, Finzi and Marinelli, who were all close advisers of the Duce. Although Matteotti's body was not found until 16 August his disappearance on 10 June led everyone to fear the worst. It was also assumed that, directly or indirectly, Mussolini was implicated. There was an explosion of anger which took Mussolini by surprise and threatened to bring his career to an end. Some of his leading ministers, including Federzoni and Gentile, were prepared to resign if he failed to remove Rossi and his associates. Protesting his innocence, Mussolini complied with their request; he also dismissed De Bono as head of the militia and appointed Federzoni as minister of the interior, hoping that this would reassure his critics that the maintenance of law and order was in safe hands. By the end of the month Dumini and his gang were under arrest.

To register their protest and isolate the Fascists, the opposition deputies decided to boycott parliament. This celebrated Aventine Secession began towards the end of June but it proved to be a serious tactical error. By remaining outside the chamber they denied themselves the opportunity to challenge every move made by the Fascists and, equally importantly, they gave the king a pretext for not intervening in their favour. Victor Emmanuel wanted representations to come in constitutional fashion from parliament itself. He was, in any case, unwilling to move against Mussolini as this would produce a dangerous political power vacuum. Liberals, the army and – most vigorously – the *ras* and the consuls of the militia announced their support for Mussolini. They used his temporary embarrassment to extract as many concessions as possible. The army, for example, insisted that the militia took an oath to the king and not just to the Duce. The moderates secured the removal of corrupt office holders and the appointment of men like Federzoni and Rocco. The radical Fascists (who prided themselves on *not* being implicated in the Matteotti murder) were able to demonstrate the indispensability of the *squadristi* and the militia in a time of crisis. Although Mussolini had recovered his nerve during the summer he faced renewed pressure in the autumn, which led the provincial intransigents to speak ever more threateningly of 'the second wave', the completion of the Fascist revolution.

One by one, Giolitti, Salandra, Orlando, Albertini, Ettore Conti of Confindustria, Alfredo Lusignoli and many others criticised the government. Mussolini decided to deny any support for 'the second wave', to pronounce the Fascist revolution over and to distance himself from the provincial *ras*. Meanwhile the crisis deepened as Balbo, who had assumed command of the militia, became involved in a libel action during which it became apparent that he had ordered attacks on socialists. He was forced to resign. This 'victimisation' of Balbo alarmed all the intransigents. Normalisation policies might compel Mussolini to sacrifice all of them. Another problem was the *memoriale* written by Rossi after he had been made a leading scapegoat in the Matteotti affair. In this testament Rossi accused the Duce of ordering the attack and other crimes against opponents. It fell into the hands of one of Mussolini's staunchest enemies, Giovanni Amendola, who published it in his newspaper on 27 December 1924. He was confident that the king would now intervene.

With General Gandolfo as Balbo's replacement there were fears that the army might absorb the militia, and faced with the prospect of dismissal many of the *ras* and consuls began to plot to safeguard their power and prestige. Mussolini had used this threat to protect his position in Rome but pressure from the moderates in the party and from the liberals had induced him to change course and advocate normalisation. As serious divisions began to appear in the PNF he had to decide quickly whether to champion the moderates or the extremists. He calculated that, at least in the short run, the consuls posed the most dangerous threat. Almost certainly he had decided to take a firm line with the opposition before the celebrated meeting with the thirty-three consuls on 31 December. The previous day, with the assistance of Federzoni and the service ministers, the cabinet had sanctioned 'necessary measures' to combat critics of the government. The army, the police and the moderates were apparently reassured by promises to pursue legal methods.[9] The 'confrontation' with the consuls, with Mussolini accepting their demands in order to preserve his leadership, was perhaps not the dramatic turning-point which some historians have suggested.

Mussolini had manoeuvred with great skill in an extremely tense situation. His offer to return to a system of single-member constituencies and the possibility of an imminent election, which he had put forward on 20 December, had created just enough hesitation on the part of moderate Fascists and liberals to prevent a combined attack on the government; his promises at the cabinet meeting on 30 December had preserved ministerial unity. It enabled him to convince the angry consuls that he was *already* determined to act 'in Fascist style', that he was still in command despite the various concessions he had deemed necessary. He completed this performance with his speech on 3 January 1925, in which he proclaimed his own personal responsibility for the crimes committed by fascism: 'I declare . . . that I, and I alone, assume the political, moral and historical responsibility for all that has happened . . . If fascism has been a criminal association . . . the responsibility for this has been mine.'[10] He challenged the deputies or anyone else to make use of Article 47 of the Constitution, which gave them the right to accuse the king's ministers and take them to the high court of justice. No one responded but many of his listeners expected the king to take action. Victor Emmanuel was astonished by Mussolini's confession of guilt but 'he did not think there was any alternative statesman who could cope with the actual situation'.[11] In his taciturn way, the king admired and even liked the Duce. So the king, the liberals and the Aventine failed to react vigorously or effectively to the threats of Mussolini. On 5 January the ironically-named *Rinascità liberale* described his speech as 'the Caporetto of the old parliamentary liberalism'.

The Matteotti crisis and the speech of 3 January were also the Caporetto of economic liberalism.[12] Alberto De Stefani, the Fascist finance minister (December 1922–July 1925), had initially won the approval of industrialists by his emphasis on reducing government influence on private enterprise. The telephone system and life insurance were privatised and many of Giolitti's schemes were dropped, such as the bill to establish compulsory unemployment insurance, a law requiring the registration of stocks and bonds in the name of the owner and a parliamentary investigation into war profits. Lower taxes and the abolition of price and rent controls, the reduction of government spending and the streamlining of state administration to combat inflation were all enthusiastically applauded by the leaders of the Confindustria. In 1924 De Stefani produced a budget surplus for the first time since the war. The reviving world economy undoubtedly improved Italy's economic prospects, enabling the Mussolini government to claim the credit for overcoming the post-war depression. Big business and the agrarians were also able to profit from the spectacular decline of Socialist and Catholic trade unions. There still remained, however, the problem of Rossoni's Fascist unions and his continuing quest for 'integral syndicalism'. This involved the creation of mixed corporations containing both employers and workers; this was viewed with alarm by the president of the Confindustria, Antonio Benni (1923–34), and its secretary-general Gino Olivetti (1919–34), who began to petition Mussolini to preserve the integrity and independence of their organisation. This basic aim was achieved with the signing of the Palazzo Chigi pact in December 1923. The Confindustria and Rossoni's Confederation of Syndical Corporations agreed to co-operate with each other but to operate as separate organisations. This agreement, personally arranged by Mussolini, virtually fell apart during the Matteotti crisis and in the months following Rossoni once again tried to impose his vision of the corporative state by instigating a series of strikes to put pressure on the industrialists. Mussolini was forced to intervene a second time and the Palazzo Vidoni agreement was signed in October 1925. Unlike the previous pact, this stated unequivocally that all labour disputes had to be resolved exclusively by the Confindustria for the employers and by Rossoni's confederation for the workers. But Rossoni had to abandon his integral syndicalism and agree to the abolition of factory councils. The government then proceeded to outlaw all strikes and established labour courts which would impose compulsory arbitration. It was clearly a victory for the industrialists and a significant contribution to the consolidation of the fascist regime after 1925.

There were no serious strikes to threaten Mussolini's rule until March 1943.[13]

The establishment of the Fascist regime

The industrialists had been successful largely because Mussolini himself was suspicious of Rossoni and the syndicalists. Rossoni was being called 'the Duce of fascist labour', and even after his defeat in the Vidoni agreement he still refused to abandon the struggle. Mussolini found this intolerable and in 1928 he broke up Rossoni's national confederation into a number of associations. Rossoni left the labour movement and agreed to serve the regime in posts of less importance. It had taken nearly ten years to bring the syndicalists under control and finally to integrate them into the regime. It took even longer to solve the much more serious problem of the *squadristi* and the intransigents of the party.

The moderates in the PNF, the ex-Nationalists and non-Fascists regarded the radicals as a continuing threat to the stability of the regime. Rejecting the accusation that they were now anachronistic, the intransigents pointed to the key role they had played in the Matteotti crisis and called for the 'second wave', the implementation of the promises made by Mussolini in his 3 January speech. They resented the presence of Federzoni as minister of the interior and deplored the appointment as minister of justice (January 1925–July 1932) of Alfredo Rocco, another ex-Nationalist. Deciding against direct confrontation, Mussolini sought to placate them by choosing Farinacci as secretary-general of the PNF. Farinacci, the *ras* of Cremona, had been threatening a 'second wave' since June 1924 and was generally regarded as the leader of the intransigents.[14] His appointment seemed to confirm the supremacy of the party over the state, but this was not Mussolini's intention. On his arrival in Rome in February 1925, the new secretary-general was allocated the task of purging and disciplining the party. The Duce shrewdly calculated that he might succeed in converting a poacher into a gamekeeper, but even if this failed – and it did – he could always ensure that Farinacci had enough rope to hang himself – and he did. Farinacci plunged into his duties with characteristic dynamism. He aimed to eliminate the remnants of parliamentary opposition, muzzle the press, 'fascistise' the civil service, destroy freemasonry and replace time-serving 'fascists of the last hour' with youthful, fanatical new recruits. Unwittingly, Farinacci laid the foundations for Mussolini's personal ascendancy and in the process he made more enemies than friends. He showed, however, a natural reluctance to curb the power of the provincial *ras* and to condemn the continuing assaults by *squadristi* on what he considered to be legitimate targets like lawyers, intellectuals and other middle-class liberals. The leader of the Aventine secession, Giovanni Amendola, was attacked in July 1925 and later died of his injuries, and in October 1925 there was the infamous 'massacre' in Florence – an episode which Mussolini particularly condemned because it took place in front of the tourists! Equally embarrassing for the regime were Farinacci's intemperate attacks on the church and the monarchy. Slowly recovering from his ulcers, the Duce realised that Farinacci was uncontrollable and that his belief in a kind of 'permanent revolution' was preventing stabilisation and threatening Mussolini's own position. Proud of his legal qualifications (acquired through plagiarism in the law faculty of Modena!), Farinacci's decision to defend Dumini and the assassins of Matteotti at their trial in Chieti gave the Duce the opportunity to replace him. He had defied strict instructions to avoid political pronouncements at the trial so in March 1926 the Grand Council dismissed him and appointed Augusto Turati secretary-general (1926–30). Farinacci and Mussolini did not meet again until 1933. As in the case of Rossoni, the Duce did not seek to destroy Farinacci. They might become useful once again and both syndicalism and *squadrismo* could be kept in reserve either as a threat or a promise.

It was Turati who finally tamed the party and subordinated it to the state. The former *ras* of Brescia, the best secretary-general the party ever had, pursued a vigorous policy of centralisation. New party statutes abolished the election of officials, who were now appointed from above. Local bosses lost most of their power, despite the frantic protests of Farinacci, and the militia was more tightly controlled under the leadership of career officers. With the possible exception of Farinacci's *Il regime fascista* and Balbo's *Corriere padano*, provincial fascist newspapers were forced to conform or else closed down.[15] The party had nearly one million members by the end of 1926. Massive purges and voluntary withdrawals took place (over 150,000 were expelled or left the

PNF by 1929) and between 1927 and 1933 no new members were admitted except those entering through the youth movements. Even so it was a mass party, which rose to one and a half million in 1933 when membership was re-opened and two and a half million by 1939.[16] Clearly it could not claim to be a vanguard party and Turati's hopes of converting it into a new ruling class became totally unrealistic.[17] The PNF was integrated into the regime and became the servant of the state. After 1927 it was no longer necessary for the Duce to send circulars to the prefects ordering them to assert their authority over all fascist party officials (see Document 7). The party constitution of December 1929 explicitly referred to the subordination of the PNF to the state. Under Turati and his successors the party became a massive bureaucracy which was rapidly becoming depoliticised. The party card became a prerequisite for a successful career; after 1933 it became compulsory for teachers and state employees. Party membership was not only an economic fact of life for the upwardly mobile middle classes, it was a ticket allowing entry into the organisations and leisure facilities of the *Dopolavoro* (see Documents 11 and 12) and other social institutions established by the PNF. Social activities like sport, organised holiday excursions, popular theatrical and musical events all proved to be the most popular aspect of party membership and also attracted the interest of the lower classes. This was *not* what Turati had in mind when he advocated the involvement of the masses in the life of the party. Although subordinate to the state, he believed the PNF had to play an active and creative part in Italian life. It was not a vision shared by Mussolini or by ministers like Federzoni and Rocco.

While Farinacci and Turati were preoccupied by party matters, Federzoni and Rocco were restructuring state institutions. They were both ex-Nationalists with a firm belief in a strong, authoritarian state. By July 1925 there was no longer a coalition government; it had become exclusively Fascist. There was no longer a free press and opposition newspapers were closed down or taken over. When the Aventine deputies sought to re-enter parliament in early 1926 they were turned away and in the autumn of that year all non-Fascist political parties and trade unions had been dissolved. It was the task of the two leading ministers to construct the institutional and legal framework for this new authoritarian state. By the time Federzoni was asked to resign in November 1926 this had been completed. They were helped, of course, by the virtual absence of any opposition but also by a series of assassination attempts on the Duce. The Socialist Tito Zaniboni's attempt on 4 November 1925 resulted in the law on the powers of the Head of Government (24 December 1925). The prime minister was no longer accountable to parliament, only to the king, and was granted virtually unlimited executive power.[18] It was not the establishment of the 'totalitarian' state which Mussolini had advocated earlier in the year but it was a giant stride in that direction. This was followed by laws against secret societies and a purge of suspect civil servants. In the following months elected mayors were replaced by appointed officials called *podestà*, which placed local government in the hands of a centralised administration. Most of the 7,000 new officials were recruited from the ranks of the old agrarian notables. 'In this way', it has been argued, 'the government paid off a debt to the agrarians who regained complete control over local affairs'.[19] After Violet Gibson's failed attempt there was no immediate response as she was obviously deranged, but five months later, in September 1926, the third attempt, by an anarchist this time, did have important repercussions. It led to the appointment of Arturo Bocchini as chief of police, a position which he held until his death in 1940. A career civil servant and a successful prefect, Bocchini was far from being a doctrinaire Fascist. He was the main architect of the 'police state' but persistently repelled moves to create a party-dominated political police along the lines of Himmler's SS. He was unable to prevent a fourth assassination attempt at the end of October, which may, in fact, have been a plot devised by dissident Fascists in Bologna. Whatever its true significance, its impact was dramatic. Mussolini himself replaced Federzoni at the interior ministry and the decree on public safety of 6 November 1926 gave the authorities wide powers to arrest suspects and dissolve political and cultural organisations. Suspects were condemned to house confinement or sent to remote regions or islands for terms of up to five years. Many intellectuals placed in *confino* became aware for the first time of the desperate existence of peasant communities in the more backward areas of the kingdom (see Document 8). Rocco's authoritarian laws *legalised* arbitrary arrest and disrespect for individual liberties. It has, however, been pointed out that such practices as *confino* were inherited from the liberal era.[20] On 25 November the 'exceptional decrees' were drawn up, reinstating the death penalty for attempts on the life of the royal family or the head of government. A Special Tribunal was set up, composed of officers from the armed services and the militia, and the political offenders brought before it were subject to military law. It was a potent deterrent, with the right to impose the death penalty, but it was responsible for only nine executions between 1927 and 1940. Its main targets were Communists and Slavs from the Trieste area. Bocchini also established the OVRA (*Opera volontaria per la repressione antifascista*), the regime's secret political police. Again, it was the threat posed by this mysterious organisation which was more important than its actual activities. Rocco, Bocchini and Mussolini himself were neither sadistic nor bloodthirsty. Indeed, after 1926 they had no need to be and with the spectacular decline in opposition they could afford to take a more relaxed attitude to the problems of law and order. The traditional legal system, even after Rocco's penal code of 1931, operated much as it had done before 1922 – and was to continue to do so after the fall of fascism.

Parliament also continued to exist but after 1926 there was only one political party, the PNF. The head of government, after the decree of December 1925, was no longer responsible to parliament. Its position as a credible institution was further weakened by the electoral law of May 1928. This provided for a single electoral list of 800 names submitted by various fascist organisations and presented to the Fascist Grand Council, who then selected 400 names which were, in turn, put before an electorate which excluded all non-fascists. This list could be accepted or rejected *en bloc*. In the 'plebiscite' of March 1929, when this new system was first introduced, there were just 137,761 no votes out of over eight and a half million! In December 1928 another law affecting the Fascist Grand Council was introduced. It was legally integrated into the state apparatus and was described as 'the supreme organ which co-ordinates and controls all the activities of the regime'. It was to draw up for the king a list of names for the posts of head of government (who also had to be the Duce of the Fascist Party) and all the ministries. In addition, it had the right to determine the succession to the throne and the extent of the royal prerogatives – claims which the king naturally deplored but equally naturally accepted after he had made his protests. This new role for the Grand Council intensified the debate over party/state relations. Just as the dismissal of Federzoni or Farinacci had been hailed as a victory by one side or the other, so this new law stirred up bitter controversy. It was all rather futile. The Grand Council rarely met to decide anything of great significance (except in July 1943) and in any case it was under the complete control of Mussolini, who summoned it, prepared the agenda and dismissed it. The true significance of this and the other laws passed or decreed since 1925 was that neither the state nor the party had emerged as the victor. It was Mussolini who had triumphed. As head of government and Duce of Fascism, he was the supreme co-ordinator, the ultimate mediator, the dictator of Fascist Italy.

Notes

1   G. Bonfanti, *Il Fascismo*, Bresicia, 1976, i, p.111.
2   A. Aquarone, *L'Organizzazione dello stato totalitario*, Turin, 1965.
3   R. De Felice, *Mussolini il fascista*, Turin, 1966, i, p.422.
4   *Ibid.*, p.150.
5   C. Duggan, *Fascism and the Mafia*, New Haven, 1989, p.124.
6   There are two excellent studies of nationalism: A. De Grand, *The Italian Nationalist Association and the Rise of Fascism in Italy*, Lincoln Nebraska, 1978; F. Gaeta, *Nazionalismo italiano*, Naples, 1965.
7   A. Lyttelton, *The Seizure of Power*, London, 1973, p.151.
8   De Felice, *Mussolini il fascista*, i, p.495.
9   Lyttelton, *Seizure of Power*, p.264.
10   The speech is in Bonfanti, *Il Fascismo*, i, pp.144–9.
11   D. Mack Smith, *Italy and its Monarchy*, New Haven, 1989, p.262.
12   D. Roberts, *The Syndicalist Tradition and Italian Fascism*, Manchester, 1979, p.234.
13   See R. Sarti, *Fascism and the Industrial Leadership*, Berkeley, 1971.
14   H. Fornari, *Mussolini's Gadfly: Roberto Farinacci*, Nashville, 1971, p.88.
15   C. Segrè, *Italo Balbo*, Berkeley, 1987, p.138.
16   M. Clark, *Modern Italy 1871–1982*, London, 1984, p.237.
17   E. Tannenbaum, *Fascism in Italy: Society and Culture 1922–45*, London, 1973, p.69.
18   C. Delzell, *Mediterranean Fascism*, pp.62–4.
19   A. De Grand, *Italian Fascism*, Lincoln, Nebraska, 1989, p.55.
20   Lyttelton, *Seizure of Power*, p.298.

4

The construction of the regime: economic and social developments

The *Decennale* of 1932

1932 was the tenth anniversary of the March on Rome. Officially it was year X of the Fascist Era because in 1926 a new calendar came into operation with year I E.F. (*Era Fascista*) beginning October 1922. The regime was determined to celebrate in grandiose fashion. With the world depression at its height, the new Italy intended to demonstrate the achievements of Fascism and its successful pursuit of a 'third way' which was neither socialist nor capitalist. It was significant that this was the year that Mussolini, with the help of Gentile, finally decided to give a full definition of Fascism in the famous article in the *Enciclopedia italiana* (see Document 9). Along with the parades and festivities of the *Decennale* there was the 'exhibition of the Fascist revolution' on the via Nazionale in Rome. Behind a modernistic facade with its huge fasces and an X on each wing of the building (devised by leading architects Mario De Renzi and Adalberto Libera to proclaim the fusion of ancient Rome with the modern world), were a series of rooms depicting each stage of the Fascist revolution from 1914 to 1922.[1] Nearly four million people passed through them over the next two years.[2] Prominent artists like Mario Sironi of the *Novecento* school helped to decorate the rooms, arrange the lighting and produce the necessary stage effects. This was Fascist propaganda at its best, impressing not only the wide-eyed workers and peasants arriving in droves but also distinguished foreigners like Le Corbusier and André Gide. The visitors moved from room to room – the editorial office of *Il Popolo d'Italia*, the heroic struggle in the war, the victory of *squadrismo* and the March on Rome – and became witnesses of what has been called a 'progressive revelation', culminating in their entry into the innermost shrine of the Fascist martyrs. It was meant to be not just an introduction to the history of the movement but a religious and mystical experience. The whole exhibition was dominated by the figure of Mussolini. The 'cult of the Duce' was everywhere apparent. This cult had developed rapidly since 1926 and its devotees were not afraid to use religious symbolism or to proclaim Mussolini as a new Messiah. Even the pope had called him a 'Man of Providence'. 'Mussolini is always right' together with 'Believe, Obey, Fight' became the slogans of the regime, and in 1930 a School of Fascist Mysticism had been established under the aegis of the party to propagate the myth of the Duce. Apart from the exaltation of the leader, the exhibition also had another important message. Put bluntly, it consigned the Fascist revolution to past history; it was now over and there would be no 'second wave'. The 'Fascists of the first hour' and the *squadristi*, the *ras* and the integral syndicalists had played their heroic part – and this had been acknowledged in the rooms of the exhibition – but they must now rest on their laurels or expect a call from Bocchini's police.

The events of the Decennale presented the regime with an opportunity to recount the triumphs of the last decade. Rocco, who lost his post in July 1932, and Federzoni (president of the senate from 1929) had successfully constructed an authoritarian state between 1925 and 1932. Their legal and political reforms had given the head of government complete control over his ministers and parliament. The opposition parties and their press, together with non-Fascist trade unions, had been eliminated. Through the Grand Council the Duce tightened his control over the party and, to some extent, over the king. Rossoni's confederation had been broken up and integral syndicalism had ceased to be a threat. The militia had been brought under control, the police had been efficiently reorganised under Bocchini and General Badoglio and the army leaders had been content to support a government which left them with considerable autonomy. During this process, of course, liberal freedoms had been ruthlessly suppressed, but for many Italians who longed for stability it was a price worth paying.

Propagandists of the regime in 1932 were swift to point out that

Italians had received much more than the establishment of law and order under a firm government. Political stability had helped to create a sound and progressive economy and the implementation of the concept of the corporative state. With greater justification they could refer to the benefits conferred by the regime's social legislation and the organisations set up by the PNF dealing with education and youth movements, the role of women, leisure activities and cultural affairs. Finally, they could produce the Lateran Pacts of 1929, which resolved the Roman question and achieved the reconciliation of church and state.

Economic policy

Just as there was never a distinguishable 'Fascist foreign policy' (see Document 10) so there was no 'Fascist economic policy' despite the rhetoric about the 'third way', the corporate state and autarchy. With her geographical position and the need to import basic raw materials, Italy could scarcely hope to become a hermit kingdom with a closed economy. Like most dictators Mussolini believed more in will power than economic theories and sought to solve intractable problems concerning the currency or the grain supply by waging 'battles'. He and his advisers, however, were always reluctant to challenge the opinions of big business and the agrarians. Integral syndicalism and integral corporativism were anathema to the *Confindustria* and its leading representatives were able to ward off threats to their independence, helped by the fact that Mussolini himself was increasingly suspicious of the schemes of Rossoni, Bottai and Ugo Spirito, the most radical of all the theorists of the corporative state. Private property and private enterprise remained largely sacrosanct, although the state did reserve the right to intervene if a crisis arose or if the national interest demanded it.

The strength of industrial and agrarian capitalism was clearly revealed shortly after the fourth (and last) congress of the PNF in June 1925. Finance minister De Stefani was under attack because he was too much of a free-trader, too hostile towards government subsidies and public works, and unable to curb inflation. He was replaced by Giuseppe Volpi, a Venetian industrialist and financier who had also been a tough governor of Tripolitania, the Italian colony in North Africa, and who became the president of the *Confindustria* in 1934. Big business had entered the Fascist government but never became truly 'Fascistised', and continued to play the key role in economic policies until 1943. The abolition of strikes in 1926, the disbanding of non-Fascist trade unions and peasant co-operatives, together with the dismantling of Rossoni's confederation in 1928 had, of course, immensely strengthened the position of the industrialists and the agrarians. On occasions, therefore, the Duce felt the need to counterbalance their power by personal interventions and by keeping alive the *possibility* of a revival of syndicalism or the implementation of integral corporativism. Two examples of this personal intervention occurred soon after Volpi's appointment.

In a speech at Pesaro on 18 August 1926 Mussolini announced his solution to the inflation problem. In this 'battle for the lira' he imposed the famous *quota novanta* (90 lira to the £), which Volpi and the business class thought grossly overvalued the currency – they argued for 120 to the pound sterling. Mussolini rejected their advice, claiming that the prestige of Italy was at stake. They had to accept this. Meanwhile, the Duce was also engaged in the 'battle for grain'. The decision to raise tariffs against the importation of foreign wheat was prompted by several considerations. To pursue a deflationary policy it was necessary not only to cut wages but also to reduce expenditure by curbing the inflow of expensive imports. This was welcome news for the progressive farmers of the Po valley, who could increase their yield and their prices in a protected home market. Protection would also help the less efficient landowners of the south and enable them to survive without modernising. Intensive farming in the north would also please industrial cartels like FIAT, who hoped to sell more tractors, and Montecatini, who would supply fertilisers. Key interest groups, whose economic and political support for the regime was crucial, would therefore be satisfied. There was also an ideological element. Fascism had long emphasised rural values and the need to prevent 'the flight from the countryside'. Ruralisation policies to ensure a social balance and promote a stable peasant population became intermingled with yet another battle, the 'battle for births'. The Duce wanted to increase the population as this would reflect the virility and vitality of the regime. As peasant households produced the largest families, it was important to prevent migration to the towns. Apart from repressive, administrative measures – which were tried but failed – a partial solution was explored in the 'battle for land reclamation', which was begun by Arrigo Serpieri as under-secretary of national economy in 1924, virtually vetoed by suspicious landowners and then resumed by him as under-secretary of agriculture (with Acerbo as minister) in 1929. Prestigious schemes like draining the Pontine marshes near Rome and the establishment of new towns like Latina and Sabauda were great achievements but tended to have more significance as propaganda and evidence of *romanità* (see p. 85) than as a solution to rural problems. Indeed, this whole question of ruralisation and the battle for births was riddled with contradictions. Fascist claims to be forward-looking and progressive, with the emphasis on modernisation in an urban setting (see Document 2 for the Futurist version), were scarcely compatible with rustic idealism. Again, an over-populated Italy with a growing number of unemployed and under-employed could do without a baby boom, despite the views of the Duce and the pope! Crudely stated, Mussolini required more soldiers and Pius XI more Catholics. The Duce constantly referred to the need to place society on a war footing, hence his interest in increasing the population and also his battle for grain, which could be seen as part of the programme for autarchy, for making Italy self-sufficient as preparation for the day when real battles had to be fought. These were ideas which had to be taken far more seriously in the course of the next decade.

Perhaps one idea which the Duce himself never took very seriously was the concept of corporativism, but as the supreme 'Editor-in-Chief' he realised its propaganda value at home and abroad, and as an astute politician he saw the tactical advantages which it offered. Much was written at the time about the origins and significance of corporations (see Documents 11 and 12). Some pointed to the medieval guilds while others emphasised the theories of the Catholic Church; in his *Quadragesimo anno* of 1931 the pope had reminded the world that it was the fortieth anniversary of Leo XIII's *Rerum Novarum*, the encyclical which contained corporativist ideas. The Fascist programme of 1919 had supported corporations (see Document 2), which had become an integral part of syndicalist doctrine and were advocated by many left-wing and trade union movements. Right-wing Nationalists like Corradini and Rocco saw them as a means to integrate labour relations within the machinery of state to eliminate class war. As minister of justice Rocco had the opportunity to implement some of his ideas in the law on Fascist trade unions in 1926. Unions were defined as legal agents of the state, strikes were forbidden, there was compulsory arbitration and labour courts were established. Only *one* organisation of workers and employers in each category of production received official recognition. It has been suggested that this legislation provided the basic framework for the construction of a corporativist state.[3] Indeed, it was in July 1926 that a ministry of corporations was created, under the Duce and with Bottai as his enthusiastic under-secretary. Unlike Rocco, Bottai was prepared to allow considerable autonomy to the corporations, but before this could be taken in hand he had the task of drawing up the celebrated Charter of Labour in 1927. For the first but not the last time he came up against the implacable hostility of the *Confindustria* towards any move which threatened their independence by imposing constraints upon managerial control over the work-force. Whereas the workers' position had been weakened, leaving them vulnerable to dictation by the state, the employers had gained in strength and had powerful allies in the government. Only if Mussolini had been ready to launch a 'battle for the corporations' would a viable corporative system have been established – and he never was really prepared to offer more than sporadic support. In the event, it was Rocco who had to produce the final version of the Charter of Labour, which emerged as a declaration of intent without the force of law, another clear victory for the industrialists. It stressed private initiative but allowed the state to intervene if this needed reinforcement or if state requirements demanded. The charter offered the workers an abundance of jam tomorrow, but this would have to await appropriate legislation. What they received almost immediately were wage cuts of between 10 and 20 per cent. It was hoped that this would enable the employers to survive the currency crisis!

In 1929 Mussolini gave up seven of his eight ministries, including corporations. Bottai now became minister and his hopes rose when a national council of corporations was set up in 1930, but the onset of the depression, the continued hostility of the industrialists and Mussolini's lukewarm attitude combined to dash them. Another blow was the alarm created by Ugo Spirito at the Ferrara conference on corporative studies in May 1932. Spirito advocated common ownership of the means of production within corporations by both capital and labour, he spoke of 'economic communism' and delivering a 'mortal blow to the concept of property'.[4] Bottai tried to mediate between Spirito and his critics, but the damage had been done and Mussolini replaced him as minister in the summer of 1932. This was an aspect of the Decennale which the Duce did not want publicised! The number of corporations had gradually been increasing and in 1934 they reached the grand total of twenty-two. It is perhaps worth noting that the first corporation to be created was the one for theatres and spectacles. The final act came in 1939 with the replacement of the old parliament by a chamber of *fasci* and corporations. The idea of dispensing with the old representational system in politics and substituting one based on occupational status had gained wide currency in the first decades of this century. The abolition of class war and the resolution of labour disputes by face-to-face meetings by employers and employees with state or party representatives as adjudicators seemed a very sensible idea. The 'plebiscite elections' of 1929 and 1934 and the new assembly of 1939 appeared to implement the corporativist aim of combining economics and politics. However, as Gaetano Salvemini wrote of corporativism 'the mountain travailed and gave birth to a mouse', and Bottai himself wrote to his son 'I performed well in a flawed system'.[5]

The great depression which struck Italy in the early 1930s did more than destroy Bottai's chances of pursuing his corporativist schemes, it removed any lingering hopes that the workers might receive some of the benefits promised by the Charter of Labour. It also made nonsense of the claim that fascism's 'third way' had rendered it immune from such crises. Official unemployment soared to over a million by 1933 and financial and industrial institutions began to face collapse. The state was forced to intervene far more vigorously than it had in the previous decade. The IMI (*Istituto mobiliare italiano*) was created in 1931 to attempt a rescue operation in the banking sector. When this proved insufficient, the IRI (*Istituto per la ricostruzione industriale* – the institute for industrial reconstruction) was set up and took over the stock holdings of banks and companies in peril. Interestingly, the ministry of corporations was totally ignored. IRI mainly benefited the large cartels, which grew even larger. By 1939 the state had a controlling interest in steel, naval construction and many other industrial sectors. It could direct economic planning and reorganisation by the use of financial inducements, as banks were no longer able to offer long-term investment. Despite assurances that private enterprise was not under threat, businessmen began to feel uneasy. This unease increased after the outbreak of the Ethiopian war in 1935 and the League of Nations' boycott. Mussolini had to rely more on trade with Germany and to develop a comprehensive autarchic programme. New taxes and price controls, import restrictions, low foreign currency reserves were regarded with dismay by Volpi and his colleagues in the *Confindustria* but while Italy was at war or preparing for war they dared not appear unpatriotic. They had to remain content with the devaluation of the lira in 1936, the increased orders for war materials and the improvement in agricultural prices. Workers enjoyed some pay rises but they were still worse off than in the late 1920s, and their consumption of a whole range of foodstuffs had declined. The middle classes became more and more dependent on posts in the bureaucracy and in the dozens of parastate organisations which proliferated after 1925. One basic reason why over two and a half million men were PNF members by 1939, why over 700,000 women had joined and one and a half million peasant women were in the *massaie rurali*, was because the party card was a passport to employment, a meal ticket (literally) or subsidised recreational activities.

Social reforms

Without the social reforms introduced earlier, these economic problems could have led to widespread protests and disorders. After 1922 the state and the PNF had addressed the problems associated with the new 'age of the masses' by establishing huge, national organisations, which by the end of the 1930s included between one third and one half of the entire population of men, women and children. In the crucial area of education and youth movements there were over eight million in the GIL (*Gioventù italiana del Littorio*, the Italian youth movement) and the GUF (*Gruppi universitari fascisti*, the fascist students' union); in the

OND (*Opera nazionale Dopolavoro*, the 'after work' or leisure organisation) there were over four million members; the PNF itself and its various auxiliaries accounted for another five million. If the militia, the corporations and various professional groups are included the total must indeed exceed twenty million out of an Italian population of forty-four million. As these organisations grew in the 1930s they provided something of a safety net for the distressed and the disenchanted. The vast bureaucracies provided employment; many of these agencies distributed relief and presented opportunities for sport and recreational activities; all organisations aimed at 'socialisation', at the integration of all groups within the regime. All members took an oath of loyalty to the Duce and were instructed to 'believe, obey and fight' but not to concern themselves with any form of political activism. Ironically, integration within the political regime, membership of the PNF or any of its offshoots was intended to *depoliticise* the population. Even in the various party headquarters notices were posted declaring 'Here we work, we do not talk politics'. This was a system which obviously ran a very serious risk of losing its dynamism and perhaps grinding to a halt. It was therefore the duty of the leaders of these organisations to convey at least the *impression* of constant activity and purposeful endeavour. Achille Starace, party secretary from 1931 to 1939, was appointed to become both 'the high priest of the cult of the Duce' and the chief choreographer of mass rallies and goose-stepping parades. He was the despair of all intelligent Fascists, but he was totally loyal to Mussolini and dedicated himself to the task of creating the illusion of movement in an increasingly static regime. The degree of regimentation he attempted to impose varied from one organisation to another and so did the effectiveness of each agency in its pursuit of socialisation policies. It is therefore necessary briefly to examine individually each of the major social reforms and to comment on the impact of the Lateran pacts of February 1929.

Education and youth movements

From the beginning *arditi*, Futurists and Fascists had constantly emphasised the need to win the support of the young generation. They adopted the song *Giovinezza* (youth) as their anthem and literally sang the praises of youth which was 'the springtime of beauty' (*primavera di bellezza*). They popularised the slogan 'make way for youth', which could also be interpreted as 'make way for us' because most of them were young men – Mussolini became the youngest prime minister and men like Balbo, Grandi and a host of others were under thirty in the early 1920s. The emphasis on youth and the emergence of a youthful elite holding high office naturally posed problems later on. The young men of 1922 were middle-aged a decade later but were unlikely to step down voluntarily to make way for immature striplings. Starace, born in 1889, attracted great ridicule by forcing himself and other Fascist notables to perform athletic feats which only confirmed the sad reality of the ageing process. Mockery and generational tensions resulted and Mussolini also had to be careful to preserve a youthful, virile image by avoiding any public participation in the more strenuous exercises prescribed by his secretary of the party.

These difficulties, however, all lay in the future and in 1923 Mussolini briskly embarked upon educational reform. He was delighted to have as his education minister Giovanni Gentile, one of Italy's most prestigious philosophers. Although Mussolini called the Gentile education act of 1923 'the most Fascist of reforms' it was widely condemned as too conservative and after Gentile's departure in July 1924 it was subjected to piecemeal dismantling. As a philosopher who believed in a spiritual communion between teachers and taught, Gentile emphasised the role of the classical *ginnasio/liceo*, the state secondary school which concentrated on Latin, philosophy and the humanities. It was the type of school which the middle classes had favoured over the preceding few decades as it offered a route to the universities and a career in the professions or the state administration. Gentile established tough state examinations, which were also open to pupils from Catholic schools. Their severity alarmed bourgeois parents, but Gentile aimed to produce an intellectual elite and deliberately sought to reduce the number of students at both secondary school and university levels – there were too many mediocre students emerging to chase too few suitable posts. Over the next few years attendance at secondary schools dropped by 100,000 (down to 237,000 in 1926) and at universities by 1,300 (down to 40,000 in 1928).[6] Gentile believed in 'fewer but better' schools and universities, and was content to see the weaker ones fall by the wayside. To the dismay of many educational reformers he was less interested in the development of technical and vocational schools, and those who attended them were virtually excluded from higher education. Gentile also left the question of elementary schooling to others – and with a 30 per cent illiteracy rate in 1921 this was clearly an important issue. Although he was anti-Catholic, Gentile did agree to the introduction of religious instruction in elementary schools and this, together with the provision for universal state examinations, did please the church leaders. The appearance of crucifixes in schoolrooms and other public institutions was a step towards better church/state relations, but the education reform as a whole was a serious disappointment. Its narrow class basis, its blatant discrimination against women, who were deemed unsuitable for the mystical process of character formation, and its neglect of technical education, were widely criticised. As it prevented social mobility it was condemned as a retrograde step which would hinder the growth of any Fascist consensus. Because it was un-Fascist it required not only drastic amendments in due course, it also needed to be supplemented by a youth movement capable of inculcating Fascist values.

In 1926 the various youth organisations promoted by the *fasci* were grouped together to form the *Opera Nazionale Balilla* (ONB). This was an ambitious attempt to create a system of youth groups to the exclusion of all others – the Catholic scouts were banned in 1928 – so that the Fascists could win the hearts, minds and bodies of the young generation. The emphasis was on 'moral and physical education' and for ten years the ONB was run by Renato Ricci, a fanatical ex-*squadrista* from Carrara although in 1929 it was formally placed within the jurisdiction of the re-named Ministry of National Education. Teachers in the state schools were expected to assist in *Balilla* activities (Balilla was the name of a legendary Genoese boy who had thrown stones at the Austrian oppressors) and most elementary schoolteachers complied. By 1934 the organisation included, apart from the original *Balilla* and *piccole italiane* (boys from eight to fourteen years and the girls' separate equivalent), the wolf cubs (boys and girls from six to eight years), the *avanguardisti* and *giovani italiane* (male and female teenagers from fourteen to seventeen) and finally young Fascists, who were enrolled in the party when they reached the age of twenty-one. Although membership of the ONB only became compulsory in 1937, peer pressure, the aspirations of upwardly mobile families and party propaganda ensured a steady enrolment, especially in the 1930s when entry into the PNF via the *leva fascista* (the passage of young Fascists into the party or the militia at age twenty-one) became the only sure way of securing employment.[7] Each member swore an oath of loyalty to the Duce and there was considerable political indoctrination for the older age groups; the 'Fascist style' was imposed on all of them at their summer camps, during their parades and public activities in the *sabato fascista* – Saturday afternoon displays in full uniform, which many of them tried to avoid! This regimentation and the wearing of uniforms did have some success in imparting a sense of party unity and national solidarity to the youth of Italy. The emphasis on physical fitness meant that drill, gymnastics and sport, together with pre-military training, played an important part in their education. Apart from elementary school-teachers and militia officers, specially trained instructors played a leading role in the ONB. After 1928 the Fascist Academy of Physical Training ran a two-year course and produced an elite corps of instructors who helped to maintain the cohesion of a vast organisation soon numbering millions. Renato Ricci was an empire-builder and was soon engaged in confrontations with the Catholic Action movement, with Carlo Scorza, the ex-*ras* of Lucca, and with De Vecchi, the *quadrumvir* who was minister of education in 1935. These jurisdictional disputes, which mainly centred on control of the young Fascists in their late teens, led to the decision in 1937 to replace the ONB with the *Gioventù Italiana del Littorio* (GIL) under the direction of the PNF.

The fascist university groups (GUF) comprised the elite of the youth movements and were always under party control. Male and female students between the ages of eighteen and twenty-eight were enrolled. Mainly middle class, they were seen as the future leaders of fascism and were granted privileges which were withheld from other groups. Apart from their weekly *Libro e Moschetto* (the book and rifle was also the slogan of fascist educationalists), they were encouraged to publish newspapers and reviews, which were often sharply critical of aspects of the regime. Experimental film groups were established and many students became involved with the newly created Cinecittà, the Italian Hollywood just outside Rome. They participated in the so-called Littorial games, intellectual competitions and debates held in various Italian cities between 1934 and 1940 where they were allowed to voice their discontent and disillusionment without fear of police intervention. It was seen by the regime as a kind of safety-valve and this free discussion was welcomed by leaders like Giuseppe Bottai, whose *Critica fascista* had expressed similar sentiments in previous years. Bottai, in fact, was appointed education minister in 1937.

Bottai inherited an educational system which had changed considerably since the Gentile reform. Fascistisation of the schools had proceeded gradually over the past decade. A loyalty oath had been imposed on all teachers in 1929 and this had been extended to university professors in 1931, when only eleven out of 1,250 had refused – thus thwarting the regime's attempt to purge these institutions because so many took the oath 'with mental reservations'. New fascist textbooks became mandatory in the early 1930s with each school year having a *libro unico*; the one written by the talented Forges-Davanzati for eleven-year olds concerning the adventures of the Balilla Vittorio won widespread acclaim and was remembered with affection in later years.[8] In 1933 the party card became compulsory for all state employees including teachers and under De Vecchi (1935-36) the whole educational system was more tightly centralised: *Balilla* activities were extended to secondary schools, religious instruction (introduced in secondary schools in 1929) was given greater emphasis and military training was introduced; 'Fascist culture' was also added to the curriculum. Bottai, who had struggled to produce the Charter of Labour in 1927, was determined to co-ordinate all educational acitivites and in 1939 drew up his School Charter. It was an attempt to break down the class barriers in the existing system and place more emphasis on science and technology. Special schools for the children of peasants and craftsmen were established to incorporate more fully the rural sector, and manual work became part of the curriculum at all levels. Bottai's aim was to democratise education and to forge the new 'Fascist man and woman', but the outbreak of war effectively doomed an experiment which had already created alarm among the conservative middle classes. His efforts to co-ordinate educational reform with the reorganised youth movements of the GIL suffered a similar fate.

Women

It was not only in the schoolroom or the youth movements that so many women and girls felt acute resentment at the subordinate roles they were expected to play by a Fascist regime which had at first seemed to promise so much. Before the war Socialist, Catholic and lay middle-class women had launched vigorous campaigns for civil rights.[9] Their contribution to the war effort seemed to reinforce their claims and there was a widespread belief that the political parties would grant them the vote and much else besides. The Fascist programme of June 1919, for instance, promised political equality (see Document 2). After 1921, however, the *squadristi* and the conservative supporters of the PNF showed pronounced hostility. Even so, Mussolini kept their hopes alive by promising the vote to various categories of women in May 1923 and then in 1925 pushed through a bill allowing them to vote in local elections, but this came to nothing in the following year when such elections were abolished. The *fasci femminili*, which sprang up in support of fascism in the 1920s and had a membership of 100,000 by 1930, were not allowed much scope. They were closely controlled by the PNF, encouraged to undertake charitable activities, to attend rallies and to help with propaganda, but they were specifically forbidden to take any political initiatives. Nor were they able to influence policies which sought to provide employment for men at the expense of women in schools, offices and the professions. A woman's workplace was the home.

The 'battle of births', Mussolini's demographic programme, clearly revealed one of the basic preoccupations of the regime – the need to boost the population figure. In 1925 an agency for maternity and infancy (ONMI) was set up and dealt, among other things, with the welfare of unmarried mothers. The following year there was a tax on celibacy, a crack-down on prostitution and the criminalisation of abortion or the advocacy of family planning. Among the more positive measures were family allowances, loans for marriages and births and the setting up of health and welfare units. In 1927 there was a vast propaganda programme involving films, public events and newspaper articles to encourage a baby boom. In all this, of course, the Vatican gave its enthusiastic support. Constant reference to family values was heard from pulpits as well as from party platforms. Both church and state condemned divorce, agreed on the outlawing of homosexuality (1931) and regarded feminism as subversive – flappers were derided as 'little men'. Because of this, the regime tolerated the existence of the Union of Catholic Women, which had more members than the fascist groups and played a much more activist role. The regime did attempt to organise women in the countryside by establishing the *massaie rurali* (rural housewives) in 1935, and women in the towns by setting up a domestic women workers' association in 1937; this was part of the party's drive to 'reach out to the people' and bring in the marginalised masses. By 1940 over two million had joined.

The regime's efforts to increase the birth-rate basically failed, and so did the attempt to exclude as many women as possible from paid employment. In 1936 it has been estimated that 28 per cent of the industrial work-force was female, 38 per cent in agriculture (the 'rural housewives' were, in fact, farm labourers!) and 34 per cent in the tertiary sector.[10] Excluding women from education was more successful, with only 25 per cent of places in the classical secondary schools being occupied by girls and only 10 per cent in the industrial schools; they provided 75 per cent, however, in the *istituti magistrali* – the teaching schools. In 1938 15 per cent of students in universities were women – up from 6 per cent in 1914, so despite the odds they had done well in this area; there were also 200 more women graduates than men from the faculties of letters, philosophy and teaching. Law and political science were hostile to women applicants. The fascist university groups (GUF) were most unwelcoming and women were only allowed to participate in the Littorial competitions in 1939. It has to be admitted that there was nothing specifically Italian or Fascist about this discrimination. It was universal and many aspects of it persist today. The two women whose names are always recorded in histories of the regime and who wielded most influence, Margherita Sarfatti and Claretta Petacci, also happened to be mistresses of Mussolini, a final sad commentary on male domination in all its aspects.

Dopolavoro

The *Opera Nazionale Dopolavoro* (OND) was established on 1 May 1925. Like the ONB, the agency co-ordinating youth movements, this organisation for the control of leisure activities was an ambitious attempt to incorporate the masses into the emerging regime. It was appropriate that this impressive piece of social engineering was suggested by an engineer, Mario Giani, a former manager of the Westinghouse plant at Vado Ligure. Edmondo Rossoni was prepared to introduce Giani's schemes for social and sporting activities into his rapidly developing syndicalist organisation. The co-operation of employers was obviously crucial as these 'after work' events required funding and the use of buildings and recreation grounds. Suspicion of Rossoni on the part of the employers seemed to be thwarting Giani's plans so he called for a national, state- sponsored scheme.[11] The OND was the answer to this appeal. Perhaps even more significant than Giani's efforts, however, was the legacy of the Socialist Party with its chambers of labour, co-operatives and leagues – many of them with mutual aid societies, communal halls and facilities for social and sporting events. The *squadristi* destroyed many of these and Rossoni and others had to start from scratch, but some were left intact and the Fascists simply took them over. Two years after its foundation Mussolini put Turati, the party secretary, in charge of the OND and he set about converting it into an integral part of the PNF. The party *federale* in the provinces would be responsible for establishing a supervisory board for the area and its members would oversee all *Dopolavoro* activities, including those sponsored by the employers. The original intention had been to use the OND to inform the workers of new industrial techniques and technological developments, but as the agency grew from 250,000 in 1926 to four million members by 1939 the emphasis was placed more and more on sport, summer camps, subsidised excursions to the sea or the mountains, cheap rail fares and welfare activities to assist families in distress. By 1936 20 per cent of urban workers had joined, only 7 per cent of rural workers, and a massive 80 per cent of employees in the state or private sectors.[12] Many of those in the last category used the clubs, shops, sports facilities and libraries provided by their own company, or their own department if they were state employees.

They were usually far superior to the average public OND establishments. Class divisions were very apparent despite attempts to use the organisation to break down barriers. On railways and steamers, for example, the lower classes were segregated and travelled in the poorest seats or cabins. Most of them did not complain. It was the first time most of them had seen the sea or the Alps or even had access to trains or boats.

Although direct political indoctrination played a very small part, the OND was seen as an instrument of propaganda, especially during the 1930s when Starace was party secretary. In the convivial atmosphere of the OND bars or during excursions the masses would be drawn into the life of the party and become aware of its successes and its problems. The regime did not expect, indeed did not want, a fanatical response. Passive acceptance of the current situation was all that was required. The OND possessed radios and while these remained a luxury item (only 300,000 in 1932 and one million in 1938) the regime hoped that communal listening would be encouraged. The radio, because of its novelty, was a great attraction and propaganda and entertainment programmes could reach the ears of millions – a great boon for both the regime and for the illiterate, unless they only spoke the local dialect. Even more popular was the cinema, and the OND acquired hundreds of projectors and sent mobile cinemas into the remoter areas. The regime was slow to realise the potential of film – perhaps it was waiting for Gentile to declare it an art form, which he did in 1939 – but became increasingly interested in its possibilities after 1934. The OND also organised travelling theatres, performances of the opera and orchestral concerts. This dissemination of so-called 'low culture' among the masses (as opposed to the 'high culture' of the intellectuals and the various academies) was an interesting experiment, despite the derision it drew from the upper classes where *'cultura dopolavoristica'* was condescendingly dismissed.

In 1937 the decision was taken to place the OND under the direct supervision of the Duce and to make it an integral part of the state apparatus. This vast organisation was needed to inject a greater sense of purpose into the life of the regime. Student leaders from GUF were invited to become involved and introduce more social and economic propaganda, but this proved a dismal failure. In 1939 the syndicalists were given nominal control over the OND in another desperate bid to galvanise the regime but it was really too late and in 1942 the party resumed control.

The OND was certainly the most popular institution of the Fascist period. It even survived the fall of Mussolini, changing its name in 1945 to the *Ente Nazionale Assistenza Lavoratori* (National Organisation for Worker Assistance). It served the regime quite well by providing an amazingly wide range of activities which diverted attention away from many economic and social problems. It helped to prevent widespread opposition. It did, however, enable opponents and critics of the regime to infiltrate its branches and meet together without attracting the attention of the police (see Document 12). The OND, despite the efforts made in the late 1930s, lacked any sense of dynamism and this was its fundamental defect once the regime had decided that it must play a more activist role. If Fascism hoped to create a forceful, militaristic society and to transform the average Italian into a new *'uomo fascista'* then the OND had not only failed to fulfil this mission, it had proved to be decidedly counter-productive. It was so popular precisely because it enabled millions of Italians to enjoy its resources without the obligation of any full commitment to Fascist ideals or practice.

The Lateran Pacts

The *Dopolavoro*, the organisation of the youth movements and the fascist party itself were all truly impressive structures, but they paled into insignificance in comparison with the Catholic Church. In his first speech as a deputy, Mussolini had made the obvious point that it was Roman, tracing its origins back almost two thousand years; it was also Catholic, which meant it was universal, with hundreds of millions of members throughout the world, and as a church it was authoritarian, hierarchical and centralised, with a clearly defined ideology. For such an institution the loss of its temporal power in Italy during the Risorgimento was disturbing and required redress, but it could *sub specie aeternitatis* be regarded as a little, local difficulty. An atheist and an anticlerical, Mussolini swiftly concluded that the church could not be swept aside like the Socialist Party or the trade unions. Soon after becoming prime minister he contacted Cardinal Gasparri and although serious negotiations did not begin for another two years, an agreement to end the cold war between church and state was already being considered. Pope and Duce had common enemies and the church welcomed the destruction of the liberal state, which had seized Rome in 1870 and forced the pope to become 'the prisoner of the Vatican'. It supported the drive against the freemasons and, above all, it supported the fascist crusade against socialism. The Vatican and the new government also had a similar approach towards the family, the role of women and a form of corporativism which would bring an end to class war. Fascism could deliver a stable, authoritarian state in which the church could flourish. It was essential to reach a form of accommodation and to avoid a clash of ideologies.

Acting the part of 'the prodigal son', Mussolini had his children baptised, married his wife in a church ceremony (1925) and placed crucifixes in schools and law courts.[13] The church was granted additional funds and the Catholic Bank of Rome was saved from collapse. The intricate negotiations which took place between 1925 and 1929 and the obstacles to an agreement have often been recounted.[14] One major obstacle was removed when the Vatican ordered Luigi Sturzo into exile and later allowed the Fascists to eliminate the PPI, the Catholic political party which he had led. Many church leaders had deplored the political activities of the populists and had regarded their trade unions and co-operatives with deep suspicion. *Squadristi* violence against such targets was painful but bearable. Much more difficult was the question of Catholic youth movements and welfare agencies. The fascist *Balilla* organisation was an obvious attempt by the new regime to control and indoctrinate the youth of Italy. The church put up a stout resistance, suspending negotiations, but had to admit defeat over the banning of the Catholic scout movement in 1928. Pius XI determined to preserve at all costs the Catholic Action organisation which he had nurtured since his election in 1922. Composed of lay Catholics but under the direct supervision of the church, Catholic Action ran youth clubs, sporting activities and numerous welfare agencies. It played an important role in education, not only taking a keen interest in the Catholic schools but also pressing for the extension of religious instruction from the elementary state schools to the secondary schools. In higher education, the jealously preserved jewel in the crown was the

Catholic University of Milan, whose degrees had been recognised at the time of the Gentile reforms, but Catholic Action was also concerned to maintain a Catholic presence in the other universities by supporting the Catholic university federation (FUCI), which had been founded back in 1896. This student organisation's main role was to combat the influence of the Fascist university groups (GUF). If Fascists saw the leaders of GUF as the future ruling class, the catholics saw FUCI in the same light. If the Vatican could ensure the survival of Catholic Action an agreement was possible.

There was still, of course, the question of the temporal power which had been at the heart of the 'Roman question' since the 1860s. The Vatican did not press for the restoration of the old Papal State, but it did demand a sovereign state to ensure the independence of the pope and to be a visible symbol to the outside world that he was master in his own house. King Victor Emmanuel III attempted to block this as he believed it would detract from his own sovereign rights, but he was eventually forced to give way. With most of the problems solved by private discussions the death of the chief government negotiator, Domenico Barone, prompted Mussolini himself to complete the talks and sign the pacts. Behind the scenes, the real hero had been the ubiquitous Father Tacchi-Venturi, whose tireless efforts had made him truly indispensable and worthy of at least a small statue somewhere in Rome.

On 11 February 1929 the Duce and Cardinal Gasparri signed the Lateran Pacts, which consisted of a treaty, a concordat and a financial convention. (For the most important terms of this agreement see Document 13). In brief, the independent sovereign state of Vatican City was established, and Article 24 of the treaty declared the territory to be neutral and inviolable. In Article 43 of the concordat the Italian state recognised Catholic Action, but their activities were to be independent of all political parties and under the direct supervision of the church authorities 'for the teaching and practice of Catholic principles'. This was a victory for the pope who also secured recognition of the Catholic Church as the sole state religion, together with the introduction of religious education into secondary schools, the legal validity of church marriages and the complete freedom of the church to pursue its spiritual duties. The Holy See recognised the Kingdom of Italy 'under the dynasty of the House of Savoy and with Rome as the capital of the Italian state'. In return Italy recognised the independent Vatican City under the sovereignty of the pope. Finally, the Vatican received generous compensation for its losses during the Risorgimento. The Roman question was thereby resolved and there would be no papal claims for lost territories or property.

Arguments about whether the pope or the Duce had won began almost immediately. To many, particularly those in democratic countries, it appeared that the pope had become the ally of Fascism, a view which Mussolini was keen to promote. The Duce made speeches – mainly to allay the disquiet of anticlerical fascists – asserting that the church was under the strict control of the state. Naturally the pope had to reply contradicting this. Pius XI was careful, however, to praise the man of providence and to thank him for granting true independence to the church. For a time, both men could congratulate themselves on the advantages gained. For the Duce it was a tremendously important propaganda coup at home and abroad. He had survived four assassination attempts before the negotiations with the Vatican had been successfully concluded, so perhaps this was a sign of divine protection. He had succeeded where Cavour and his successors had all failed. Catholics and conservatives everywhere saluted him. He had, nevertheless, granted wide powers to the church and guaranteed its independence, and unless he violated the Lateran Pacts he had sanctioned the existence of a state within the state, making it impossible for him to claim totalitarian power over the Italians. Pius XI had been forced to make concessions but had secured his essential aims – independence and international recognition of the Vatican City, financial security, and the preservation of Catholic Action. The church was now in a position to reconquer Italy for Christianity.

The first major conflict came in 1931. Predictably it concerned Catholic Action, whose members were accused of forming secret political groups with the assistance of ex-Populists, of creating trade unions and of organising sporting activities. At the end of May an order was issued closing down all the youth clubs and offices used by Catholic Action, including those of the Catholic students belonging to FUCI. The pope replied on 29 June 1931 with the encyclical *Non abbiamo bisogno*, which was published in

several languages and distributed abroad.[15] It denied all the
accusations and attacked the fascists' attempts to monopolise
education and to interfere with the natural rights of the family.
Referring to the oaths of loyalty being demanded, the pope
realised that to refuse would bring economic disaster and ruin
careers, so he advised taking the oath with the mental reservation
'provided this does not conflict with the laws of God and the
church' or 'provided this does not conflict with the duties of a
good Christian'. He followed this up later with a threat to issue a
public condemnation of Fascism. Father Tacchi-Venturi once
again acted as mediator and a compromise was devised and
incorporated in the September Accords of 1931. The state would
recognise Catholic Action but only in 'essentially diocesan' form;
its leaders were to be appointed by bishops and not to be elected,
and it must abstain from politics and dissolve all trade union or
professional groups. Ex-Populists were forbidden to join and
Catholic Action was prohibited from sponsoring or organising
any sporting activity. It was, however, allowed to engage in
activities which were specifically religious. Most significant for
the future, the Catholic student federation FUCI was permitted to
continue to serve the educational and religious needs of its
members.

Relations improved after 1931 until the introduction of the
racial laws in 1938 and the ever closer links with Nazi Germany
forced the pope to voice his public disquiet over events in Italy
and central Europe. By then, foreign policy had come to domi-
nate the thoughts and actions of the Duce. He had often declared
that Italy was a nation permanently mobilised for war. After 1935
he unwisely decided to prove the validity of this boastful assertion and destroyed the regime in the process.

Notes

1   E. Gentile, *Il Culto del Littorio*, Bari, 1993, p. 218.
2   M. Stone, 'Staging fascism: the exhibition of the fascist revolution',
Journal of Contemporary History, 28, 1993, p. 233.
3   A. De Grand, *Italian Fascism*, Lincoln, Nebraska, 1989, p. 69.
4   B. Guerri, *Giuseppe Bottai: un fascista critico*, Milan, 1976, p. 116.
5   *Ibid.*, p. 245.
6   De Grand, *Italian Fascism*, p. 49.

7 D. De Masi, *PNF: Manuale di educazione fascista*, Rome, 1977, p. 95.

8 E. Wiskemann, *Fascism in Italy: Its Development and Influence*, London, 1969, p. 39.

9 See the excellent treatment of this topic in V. De Grazia, *How Fascism Ruled Women: Italy 1922–45*, Berkeley, 1992.

10 P. Cannistraro (ed.), *Historical Dictionary of Fascist Italy*, Westport, 1982, pp. 202–4.

11 V. De Grazia, *The Culture of Consent: Mass Organisation of Leisure*, Cambridge, 1981, pp. 24–7, 31–2.

12 *Ibid.*, p. 55.

13 M. Clark, *Modern Italy 1871–1987*, London, 1984, p. 254.

14 The best recent account is J. Pollard, *The Vatican and Italian Fascism 1929–32*, Cambridge, 1985.

15 The text is in G. Bonfanti, *Il Fascismo*, Brescia, 1976, ii, pp. 93–7.

5

The search for an ideology: intellectuals, propaganda and racism

The Manifesto of the Fascist intellectuals, 21 April 1925

Equipped with cudgels, castor oil and even more lethal weapons, the early fascists seemed to be the very embodiment of mindless brutality. Mussolini and his followers proclaimed that actions spoke louder than words and Balbo and Grandi praised the ruthless violence of the *squadristi*. Terror tactics were more effective than argument and persuasion in dealing with opponents and far less time-consuming. Student activists could appreciate Gino Baroncini's slogan that 'one bomb is worth a hundred lectures'. It was scarcely surprising, therefore, that fascism was identified as an anti-intellectual movement and its triumph after 1922 as a victory for brawn over brain. What does seem incredible is that the judicious Guiseppe Bottai could, in March 1924, describe the advent of Fascism as 'the revolution of the intellectuals'.

His argument was that 'the harsh necessity of the anti-Bolshevik struggle' compelled the Fascists to take stern measures and also prevented them from expressing their ideas – 'you cannot talk philosophy with the enemy at the gates'.[1] He insisted that the movement did have intellectual origins, which were only temporarily obscured by the methods that had to be adopted to liberate Italy from the tyranny of Marxism. As Bottai was one of the first to admit, Fascism suffered not from the lack of ideas but from too many. Despite their rhetoric and pronounced hostility towards the intellectuals of the old liberal establishment, Futurists, syndicalists, ex-socialists and even the *ras* professed an ideology and invariably had access to a newspaper where their views could be expressed. After the conquest of power one of the major problems was the formulation of an ideology from the bewildering array of distinct ideologies within the fascist movement. The influx of Nationalists in 1923, together with other conservative elements from the urban and agrarian middle classes, gave added impetus to the quest but also increased the difficulties of reaching any ideological consensus.

Mussolini, always intent upon keeping his options open, was reluctant to define his own ideological position with any great precision or to align himself with any specific intellectual tendencies. During his first two years as prime minister he was in any case more preoccupied with consolidating his power and surviving the Matteotti crisis. It was fortunate that he had been able to secure the services of Gentile, not only as education minister but also as chief ideologue. Gentile, as philosopher, minister and friend of the Duce, naturally had a wide circle of willing accomplices in the academic world. Marinetti's bid to promote Futurism in 1923 (his Manifesto in defence of *italianità*) was largely ignored, allowing Gentile to proceed with his attempts to win the support of the intellectual establishment. This became urgent for two reasons. The popularity and respectability of the government declined disastrously as a result of the Matteotti affair; secondly, with his speech of 3 January 1925 and his pledge to establish 'totalitarian' controls, Mussolini needed to present some ideological justification for this new regime.

It was therefore no coincidence that towards the end of March 1925 a congress of Fascist intellectuals was held at Bologna, with Gentile presiding. It was significant that Farinacci, the intransigent *ras* of Cremona and the new party secretary, sent a message of greeting: 'The impressive gathering at Bologna shows Italy and the world that Fascism besides having faith and muscle also has a brain'.[2] It revealed that even *squadristi* realised the importance of what the Communist leader Antonio Gramsci called cultural hegemony – the diffusion of new ideas throughout society to establish a new orthodoxy and to consolidate the power of a new elite in a new regime.[3] Gentile was very cautious about offering exact definitions and spoke vaguely of mysticism and intuition. The main object of bringing together over two hundred intellectuals was to prove that Fascism and culture were not antithetical; in fact, the congress asserted that without Fascism there could be no true culture. This was the message of their manifesto published on 21 April 1925 (21 April was the *Natale di Roma*, the date when Rome was supposedly founded and which became one of the regime's 'holy days' in place of the socialists' May Day).

On 1 May came the reply of the anti-Fascist intellectuals, a counter-manifesto organised by Gentile's former friend, the philosopher Benedetto Croce. It was signed by an impressive number of leading academics and creative artists. It ridiculed the bizarre and conflicting ideas of Gentile's 'schoolboy's exercise' and declared Fascism and culture incompatible. This was a setback for the regime, but there was no official retaliation. Croce was allowed to continue to publish his periodical *La Critica*, perhaps because it posed no threat, perhaps because it enabled the Duce to show the outside world that he tolerated intellectual freedom. Gentile was undeterred and was soon engaged in compiling the Italian Encyclopaedia.

This mammoth undertaking, conceived by the industrialist Giovanni Treccani in 1925, won the backing of the king and the Duce. It was an impressive work of scholarship, with contributions from over two thousand Italian and foreign experts (including eighty-five signatories of Croce's manifesto!), but it was also equally impressive as a work of propaganda. More effectively than the Bologna congress, it emphasised the regime's support for cultural activities. Gentile and Mussolini finally committed themselves to a definition of Fascism in their famous entry of 1932 (see Document 9). The encyclopaedia was, however, as much a celebration of Italian achievements as of Fascist successes, but this only enhanced its propaganda value. Like the existence of *La Critica*, it revealed a regime strong enough to permit some freedom of expression, but in confronting the problems of organising what has been called 'high culture' and 'low culture' in a mass society the PNF and the state realised the need for closer controls.

Indeed, at the last PNF congress in June 1925 the decision was taken to establish a National Fascist Institute of Culture.[4] With ninety-four sections in the provinces, the institute planned to hold conferences, free concerts, language courses and sponsor museum visits and publications. This dissemination of 'low culture' would link up with the educational activities of the *Balilla* and the leisure pursuits of the *Dopolavoro*. The institute claimed

200,000 members by 1941 but only a small percentage were workers and peasants. Predictably, it was the middle classes who took advantage of the opportunities on offer. On a higher plane, the Royal Academy of Italy was announced in 1926, but not inaugurated by the Duce until 1929. The aim was to 'promote and co-ordinate Italian intellectual activity' and its sixty members were handsomely paid, given free rail travel and a dress uniform. It proved successful in attracting most leading intellectuals and incorporating them into the regime. Guglielmo Marconi became its president in 1930 and other notable academicians included Luigi Pirandello, Enrico Fermi, D'Annunzio, Gentile, Marinetti and Pietro Mascagni. This was another astute propaganda coup for the regime, which, incidentally, clearly indicated that Fascist Italy, unlike Nazi Germany, did not force into exile the majority of its intellectual elite.

The Fascists did anticipate the Nazi policy of *Gleichschaltung*, however, by taking over existing academies and societies, but they did so in a much more leisurely fashion – the prestigious *Accademia dei Lincei* being absorbed by the Royal Academy as late as 1939. La Scala of Milan was taken over in 1923 and the Dante Alighieri Society in 1929. The Nazis were able to move so swiftly not only because they possessed a much more dynamic leadership with a clearly defined ideology, but because they had more than a decade in opposition in which to devise and develop their propaganda techniques and much else besides. The Fascists had less than four years from the founding of the movement to the appointment of Mussolini as prime minister in 1922. This partly explains why Mussolini, despite or because of his obsession with the newspaper press as an instrument of propaganda, failed at first to grasp the significance of the radio and the cinema. It was true that Marconi alerted the Duce to the political advantages of a radio network and that in 1924 the URI (*Unione Radiofonica Italiana*) was set up, but it was only in the next decade that it was more fully exploited and that the regime attempted to mass produce wireless sets (there were still only one million sets by 1939, in a population of forty-four million). Also in 1924 the *Istituto Nazionale LUCE (L'Unione Cinematografica Educativa)* was established and became a state agency producing newsreels, which became a compulsory part of every cinema performance in 1926. But, like the radio, the propaganda potential was only fully realised some years later. Most intellectuals regarded the new mass media with grave suspicion or even contempt.

What the regime was attempting to achieve was greater control over all forms of creative activity, including journalism, the professions and all aspects of education. In 1928 the National Confederation of Fascist Syndicates of Professions and Artists was created and two years later the *Corporazione dello Spettacolo*, which brought together all those engaged in what could loosely be called the performing arts, which included the opera, the theatre, the cinema and sport. In 1931 it was the turn of the artists, writers, architects and the professions to join the corporation of *Professionisti e degli artisti*. Along with all this regimentation came the oath-taking – oaths of loyalty being demanded of all state school teachers in 1929 and university professors in 1931. Officially at least, all intellectuals and members of the professions could only pursue a successful public career if they had joined a corporation, sworn an oath of loyalty or entered the PNF. In other words, apart from a few exceptions (churchmen, army generals, Communist prisoners, Croce and other independents) the middle classes had been formally integrated into the fascist regime. Many – like dentists or accountants – must have puzzled over the exact implications of their new Fascist status, but others, such as ancient historians or archaeologists, clearly understood what was expected of them.

Romanità

Fascist propaganda and rhetoric cannot be fully understood without reference to the regime's growing obsession with ancient Rome. There was, of course, nothing new in the tendency to identify with the grandeur of the Roman Empire. Names such as the Roman Catholic Church, the Holy Roman Empire and Romania give clear evidence of this. Scholars and statesmen had for centuries regarded ancient Rome as the bedrock of European civilisation. Everywhere its ruins were a silent testimony to past greatness, and when the city of Rome became the capital of a unified peninsula in 1870 modern Italians inherited the 'myth of Rome'. For only the second time in history there was a unified Italy; the temptation was to emulate the achievements of the Romans. In elementary and secondary schools Roman history was taught as part of Italian history and a classical education was indispensable for all those entering the bourgeois ruling elite. Nationalists and imperialists naturally gave their full support.

In condemning the old liberal establishment, Fascists might have been expected to attack this *romanità* and the Futurists certainly did – they had to live up to their name. Mussolini and his fellow Fascists had adopted a name which virtually compelled them to emphasise the Roman past. The *fasces* (*fascio littorio*) became the symbol of the movement and then the emblem of the Fascist state. It appeared on the coinage and on stamps in 1923 and a decree law of December 1926 placed it on every government building. In 1929 it was incorporated into a new coat of arms for the state.[5] The *fasces* represented order and discipline, 'Roman virtues' which Catholics, Nationalists and classically educated conservatives found reassuring. The wolf and the eagle were other symbols which appeared during the parades of the *Balilla* and the militia. New buildings were obviously influenced by classical models; even the so-called 'rational architects' like Giuseppe Pagano and Guiseppe Terragni, who deplored what they called 'monumental rhetoric', tried to blend ancient and modern styles.[6] Marcello Piacentini, who became the Duce's favourite architect after 1937, was committed to a much more uncompromising 'imperial style'. His Foro Mussolini (now the Foro Italico) and some of the early structures of the *Esposizione Universale Di Roma* (EUR, the new Rome built to house the great exhibition of 1942, which was never held) were unmistakably Roman with their columns, arches and statues.

What was required by the propagandists of the regime, however, was a more coherent vision of *romanità* in all its forms. Otherwise, the Roman salute and the *passo romano* (the goose-step), the mass choreography in ancient amphitheatres or modern stadiums and the elaborate ceremonial on 21 April (*Natale di Roma*), might be misunderstood. It was important to view them not as isolated episodes or the eccentric whims of Starace or the Duce, but as integral parts of the very fabric of the regime. The daunting task of formulating what has been called a 'coherent fascist classicism' initially fell upon the Institute of Roman Studies, established by Carlo Paluzzi in 1925.[7] He and his colleagues were already sympathetic towards fascism, and their publications, including their review *Roma*, were a combination of scholarship and propaganda. They helped to give legitimacy to fascist ideology by indicating that its origins lay in the glorious past of the Italic people who constructed the Roman Empire. The Fascist regime represented the triumphant rebirth of the genius of this talented race. It was, however, Pietro De Francisci, the professor of Roman law at Rome University, who took this further and emerged as the high priest of *romanità*.[8] In 1935, with the backing of the Duce and Bottai, he became rector of Rome University and president of the National Institute of Fascist Culture, a body charged with the task of taking culture to the people. With its wide programme of lectures and courses throughout the nation the theorists of *romanità* were able to reach a much wider public than those who read *Roma* or attended De Francisci's law lectures. Emphasis on the heroic virtues of the Italic race perhaps helped to provide some justification for the outbreak of racism and anti-semitism in the late 1930s.

Prompted by the propagandists, it became increasingly possible to discern parallels between ancient Rome and the Fascist regime. The battle for wheat and the draining of the Pontine marshes to provide land for war veterans seemed to recall the policies of Julius Caesar. It was Caesar who had ended the civil wars as the Duce had done in 1922. This was followed by the rebuilding of Rome and the establishment of a *pax romana* under Augustus after the defeat of his rivals, policies being pursued by the Duce. Colonisation in Africa, the attempt to control the Adriatic and the Mediterranean (*mare nostrum*) and the creation of an invincible army were all contemporary themes which had obvious precedents in the past. The conclusion to be drawn was that the Duce was the reincarnation of both Caesar *and* Augustus. The next step, at least for the School of Fascist Mysticism, was to re-establish emperor worship – the cult of the Duce.

The setting for the re-enactment of this compelling drama was also crucial. Fortunately, Italy and Rome in particular possessed an abundance of monumental ruins to serve this purpose. It was nevertheless essential to clear away the clutter which surrounded so many of them, to excavate and to open up new vistas of imperial grandeur. As early as 1926 Gaetano Polverelli, the head of the press office, suggested converting the tomb of Augustus into a temple of Fascism, and later large tracts of medieval Rome were demolished to push through the via dei Fori Imperiali to link the Colosseum with the Capitol (and the Duce's residence in the Palazzo Venezia). This gave a tremendous impetus to archaeological excavation, some of it valuable, some of it disastrous.

In case this vast exercise in the cause of *romanità*, Fascist ideology and the cult of the Duce had not achieved all its goals, the regime prepared another great exhibition. During the *Decennale* of 1932 plans were drawn up for the celebration of the two thousandth anniversary of the birth of Augustus (so much for Hitler's thousand-year Reich!). Under the direction of professor Giulio Giglioli teams of experts set to work to produce the *Mostra Augustea della Romanità* which duly opened in 1937. Different sections portrayed the origins and the conquests of Rome, the life of Augustus, the structure of the Roman army and the other institutions of the imperial period. Driving home the main point of the exhibition was the section called 'Fascism and *Romanità*'. Visitors entering the exhibition read the Duce's words calling upon them to ensure that the glories of the past were surpassed by the glories of the future. As in 1932, the *Dopolavoro*, the *Gioventù Italiana del Littorio*, the PNF, the militia, the GUF and the many fascist institutes all worked hard to secure a mass attendance. Over one million people visited the exhibition and those who witnessed the closing ceremonies saw the Duce/ Augustus presented with a live eagle. In 1937 there was no escape from *romanità* even for those retreating to the cinema. The main feature film was the historical epic by Carmine Gallone *Scipione l' Africano* – an obvious reference both to ancient Rome and the recent conquest of Ethiopia. 1937 was also the year in which the Ministry of Popular Culture was established and the year in which the Duce visited the Third Reich and came away an impressed but troubled man.

Propaganda

At first sight it seems surprising that it took so long for the regime to establish a propaganda apparatus that even remotely resembled the formidable machine set in motion by Goebbels. The reason for this is quite simple. It was not necessary. State controls and social controls imposed after 1925 appeared to be more than sufficient. Bocchini's police, the OVRA, the militia, the *carabinieri* and the army could enforce the laws sponsored by Federzoni and

Rocco. Within the authoritarian state the security of society was guaranteed and this was welcomed by the majority of Italians. The 10,000 or so activist anti-fascists, scattered and divided, were no serious threat to stability. On the more positive side, the PNF and the state created national organisations like the *Balilla*, the *Dopolavoro* and the Fascist Institute of Culture, which not only exerted social control but also disseminated propaganda. These agencies never inspired wild enthusiasm but their activities helped to make the regime acceptable even in the depression years. With organised labour under control and the intellectuals and professional groups under close supervision, there seemed to be no urgency about setting up an elaborate propaganda organisation.

There was, from the beginning, the press office of the prime minister under Cesare Rossi, the close associate of the Duce. It had two sections, one dealing with Italian and the other with foreign newspapers and the state-controlled news agency *Agenzia Stefani*. Mussolini himself had risen to political prominence as a highly talented journalist and editor and he continued to take a close personal interest in the press, convinced that newspapers were the key to any propagandist success. Rossi and his successors imposed press censorship and this continued even after the last opposition newspaper had been closed down or taken over in 1926. Editors were forbidden to print news about crime, financial or sexual scandals, traffic accidents or indeed anything that suggested that the regime had problems. Government subsidies were paid to editors and journalists but the newspapers did remain in private hands; by the late 1920s, however, their staff were expected to become members of the Fascist union of journalists. The press office told editors what to print, sending them the comments they were expected to make after a speech by the Duce or in the aftermath of some particular event. No foreign news was to be published without permission and foreign newspapers were rigidly excluded; this accounts for the growing popularity of the Vatican's *Osservatore Romano*, with its independent views and extracts from the foreign press. In the early 1930s Gaetano Polverelli took charge of the press office and imposed strict regimentation of all journalists. There was much greater emphasis on the cult of the Duce. It was forbidden to mention any illnesses suffered by Mussolini, his birthday was to be ignored as was the fact that he had become a grandfather – the Duce must possess eternal youth! He must also be photographed and portrayed not only as a statesman and warrior but as a man of the people, gathering in the harvest, visiting schools and maternity wards. He was often featured driving cars, riding horses, sitting in aeroplanes (although he only received his pilot's licence in 1939) and even taming lions. Rigorously excluded was all mention of the depression, rural unrest and unpleasant events abroad such as the assassination of King Alexander – he may have been a despised Yugoslav (and killed by terrorists trained in Italy) but he was a ruler and this method of disposing of him was not to be encouraged.

The character of the press office changed even more dramatically with the appointment of Galeazzo Ciano in 1933. The son of Costanzo Ciano, designated by Mussolini as his eventual successor, and the husband of the Duce's daughter Edda, this young man of thirty took his place in the Fascist leadership and remained there until shot on the orders of his father-in-law in 1944. Goebbels visited Rome in 1933 and was not terribly impressed by the regime's propaganda apparatus. Bottai's *Critica Fascista* was also pressing for a more systematic approach. Radio and the cinema had to be taken more seriously and in September 1934 the press office was replaced by the Undersecretariat for Press and Progaganda, and Ciano attempted to supervise not only radio and cinema but also music, the theatre and tourism. In June 1935 Ciano's organisation became a Ministry for Press and Propaganda and all the media under its control were mobilised to present the Italian case in the Ethiopian question. Everything was subordinated to this one aim and the coverage of the preparation for war and the conduct of the war itself were perhaps the regime's greatest propaganda triumph. Ciano himself went off to participate in the war and left his undersecretary Dino Alfieri to orchestrate this massive effort. Roberto Forges Davanzati became a household name with his radio programme '*Cronache del Regime*', which kept listeners informed about the great events of the day and the activities of the leaders. His calm but authoritative voice proved incredibly convincing and his death in 1936 was a sad loss to the regime. There were carefully staged events like the Duce's speech declaring war in October 1935 from the famous balcony of the Palazzo Venezia before an immense crowd and heard by a million or so radio listeners (although there were only around half a million sets, communal listening created a vast audience); there was the *Giornata della Fede* on 18 December 1935 when the women of Italy from the royal family down to the poorest peasant housewife presented their gold wedding rings to be melted down as part of the war effort. Why a country 'permanently prepared for war' needed to resort to such measures was studiously ignored. When the League of Nations imposed economic sanctions, the propagandists could claim that Italy was fighting not hordes of backward tribesmen but virtually the whole world. It was undoubtedly the most popular war ever fought by Italians and the themes of *romanità*, of the civilising mission of a great imperial power and of the missionary campaign of the Catholic Church could all be combined. It enhanced the prestige of the regime, at least within Italy, and raised Mussolini's popularity and the cult of the Duce to new heights.

To preserve the momentum and to fulfil the programme of 'reaching out to the people' the name of the ministry was changed in May 1937 to Ministry of Popular Culture, or Minculpop as it tended to be called. This was run by Dino Alfieri, who had become minister after Ciano had been transferred to foreign affairs. Its staff was increased from just under 200 to over 800, many of the new officials coming from the foreign ministry. It was a clear sign of the increasing importance of foreign policy and of the need to illustrate the advantages of friendship with Nazi Germany. The regime now appeared much more bellicose but the majority of Italians clearly were not; they remained satisfied with the conclusion of the successful colonial war in Africa.

It was the duty of Starace and the PNF to galvanise Italians into action and for the machinery of propaganda to support this effort. Starace's attempts to revitalise the party and the nation were sadly ineffective. The so-called 'anti-*lei*' campaign, for example, was a disaster. Instead of using the normal, polite form of address Italians were ordered to use '*voi*'; '*lei*' was declared un-Italian and a sign of servility dating back to the Spanish domination – and this despite the fact that in Naples and the south, which were the most 'Spanish' areas, 'voi' was traditionally used. The Neapolitan Croce, to show his disgust at Starace's buffoonery, adopted '*lei*' as his form of speech. The abolition of the handshake and the substitution of the Roman salute was greeted with a mixture of irritation and hilarity, the introduction of the *passo romano* as an unwelcome German import. Alfieri was pro-German and later became Italian ambassador in Berlin (in May 1940 and at Hitler's request), but even he thought Starace's initiatives ill advised.

Bottai also was unhappy about these developments. He approved of a well-directed propaganda programme designed to produce 'real fascists' but he opposed rigid controls and excessive regimentation. He welcomed new ideas and constructive criticism of existing practices; his own *Critica Fascista* had often led the way, although it had become less adventurous in the 1930s. When he became minister of national education in 1936 he was determined to protect the educational system and the cultural establishment from the interference of men like Starace and Alfieri. Losing the *Balilla* to the party secretary when it became the GIL only strengthened his determination to prevent further encroachments. His creation of an office for contemporary art within his ministry was part of his attempt to establish dialogue between the exponents of traditional and modern art. Farinacci had awarded the Cremona Prize to promote 'Fascist art' so Bottai established the Bergamo Prize to reward modern artists. There had, indeed, been conflict between Fascist leaders who supported Futurism, the 'Novecento' style or avant-garde modern art. Mussolini himself became involved in this through the influence of his talented Jewish mistress Margherita Sarfatti. She was the art editor for *Il Popolo d'Italia*, director of the party journal *Gerarchia* and a biographer of the Duce (*Dux* was published in 1926); she helped to found the Novecento art group in Milan and persuaded the Duce to give a speech at the first exhibition held in 1926 (it included art by notable figures such as Carlo Carrà, Giorgio Morandi, Mario Sironi and Gino Severini), but Mussolini was never really committed and when their relationship ended in the early 1930s his interest waned and his preference for more traditional and 'imperial' art and architecture became apparent. As Bottai realised, faction fights with art as a weapon and patronage as a means to secure political loyalty were a venerable tradition in Italy. Nor was the age-old conflict between town and country absent in the fascist period. Massimo Bontempelli, the poet, editor and founder of the periodical

Novecento, helped to promote the so-called *Stracittà* movement, which emphasised urban values and modernism. This was opposed by Curzio Malaparte and Ardengo Soffici, who praised the traditionalism of the provinces and called their movement '*Strapaese*'. So 'superurbanism' confronted 'superruralism' or, in political terms, urban Fascists confronted the *squadristi*. For the uninitiated this struggle for cultural supremacy was all very confusing, but at least it preserved some vitality and prevented the imposition of an officially approved art form.

Bottai was acutely conscious of the wealth of talent in contemporary Italy which was not being intelligently exploited by Alfieri and Alessandro Pavolini, who ran the propaganda machine from 1936 to 1943. There were, it was true, some notable successes. Millions of Italians flocked to the cinema in the 1930s where they could enjoy escapist films of the famous 'white telephone' variety (comedies and social drama depicting the high life with all its luxurious accompaniments), the latest Hollywood productions (censored and increasingly restricted as autarchy began to bite), together with westerns and historical romances. But audiences had to watch the newsreels and documentaries of LUCE and some propagandist feature films, a few of which like Alessandro Blasetti's *Vecchia Guardia* – set in the period of *squadrismo* before the March on Rome – *Luciano Serra, pilota* and Carmine Gallone's *Scipione l'Africano* proved to be both popular and well received by critics. The regime began to take a much greater interest in filmmaking, providing funds, appointing Luigi Freddi as director general for cinematography and establishing an experimental centre where students from GUF could study. In 1937 the Duce personally opened Cinecittà just outside Rome, and his son Vittorio played an active part both in the making of films and writing about them. Two reviews, *Cinema* and *Bianco e Nero*, involved young students like Michelangelo Antonioni and Luchino Visconti, who, together with Vittorio De Sica and Roberto Rossellini, began to plan and make the neo-realist films which made the Italian cinema world famous in the post-war period. This development, however, was to a large extent opposed by the propagandists, who preferred illusion to realism – a view probably supported by most Italians.

In the 1930s Italians not only discovered the cinema but for the first time became widely involved in sport. It featured in newsreels, on the radio and in newspapers. It was encouraged in the *Balilla* and the *Dopolavoro* and most of those who did not participate became ardent spectators. With the regime's emphasis on youth and physical fitness the party propagandists quickly saw the advantages of identifying Fascism with sport. Football mania swept Italy, especially after hosting and winning the World Cup in 1934, winning again in 1938 and becoming Olympic champions in 1936. Cycling, motor racing and aerial feats like Balbo's formation flights across the Atlantic also aroused intense enthusiasm. Fascists shared the Futurists' love of speed and veneration for machines (see Document 4). The new Fascist man seemed to be personified in Primo Carnera, the world heavyweight champion from 1933 to 1935, and the gold medallists in the Olympics.[9] The masses were entranced and involved and the regime gained prestige. A virile nation was emerging, and if necessary these skills and energies could be channelled into war, the sport of kings.

The regime was successful in promoting and staging sport as a form of mass culture and social control. It was less fortunate in its attempts to create a Fascist literary intelligentsia capable of influencing both high and low culture. Luigi Pirandello, the internationally acclaimed dramatist, and D'Annunzio had supported Fascism but the young generation regarded them with indifference and, in any case, both were dead by 1938. Bottai realised that idealistic young Fascists were being frustrated by the activities of Minculpop and the sordid realities of party life. When their suggestions for reform or a return to 'real Fascism' were ignored or punished, many of them began their 'long voyage' through Fascism to anti-Fascism as described in Ruggero Zangrandi's classic *Il lungo viaggio attraverso il fascismo* (1962). Bottai sought to prevent this by taking their criticisms seriously and by arguing for a relaxation of censorship and party control. In 1940 he founded his review *Primato* and opened its pages to disenchanted Fascists and non-Fascists. Among its contributors were the poets Giuseppe Ungaretti, Eugenio Montale and Salvatore Quasimodo, who had attempted to isolate themselves from politics and the cynicism and hypocrisy of everyday life – these were the aptly named 'hermetic poets'. Cesare Pavese, who was beginning to attract attention as an introspective neo-realist novelist, also wrote for *Primato*, but like his equally talented fellow writers Elio Vittorini and Vasco Pratolini, growing distrust of the regime vitiated Bottai's efforts to convince him that fascism could be reinvigorated.[10] Bottai did his best to win them over, to condemn the assumption that literature and propaganda were synonymous and to deplore the regime's exclusion of foreign authors. But Bottai had to admit defeat and the coming of war led Pavolini and Minculpop to adopt an increasingly assertive and bellicose propaganda campaign. Bottai arrived at the stark conclusion that it was Mussolini himself who prevented the realisation of an authentic Fascist regime.[11] The cult of the Duce had replaced Fascism. It was another three years before Bottai decided to move against a man for whom he still felt considerable affection and loyalty.

Racism

To their eternal discredit, Mussolini and his ministers, Bottai included, decided to embark upon a programme of racial discrimination in the late 1930s. This was surprising for several reasons. Mussolini had often poured scorn on the racial theories of the Nazis, dismissing them as 'unscientific' and 'ridiculous'.[12] Official fascist doctrine excluded anti-Semitism until 1938. In any case, there were less than 50,000 Jews in Italy, all well assimilated. Many of them had fought in the war, were intensely patriotic and had joined the PNF. The Jews of Ferrara, the subject of Giorgio Bassani's *The Garden of the Finzi-Continis* (1962), were well established and well respected and very typical of communities all over Italy. There was an influx of a few thousand foreign Jews fleeing persecution but they presented no problem. Italians seemed remarkably free from racial prejudice and the Vatican discouraged any form of racial anti-Semitism within the Catholic Church. There were, of course, some Nationalists and Fascists who held racial views. Three of the most significant were Giovanni Preziosi, Telesio Interlandi and Farinacci. The ex-priest Preziosi was a firm believer in an international Jewish conspiracy; in 1920 he published an Italian edition of the infamous forgery the *Protocols of the Elders of Zion*, and developed his theories in journals which he controlled such as *La Vita Italiana*. His views, however, were largely ignored by the party until the late 1930s. His close links with Farinacci, a much more robust populariser of anti-Jewish myths, made him a potentially dangerous figure. Interlandi was, like Preziosi, a journalist with extreme views on most aspects of life and in 1924 he established *Il Tevere* which became outspokenly anti-Semitic. It is important to note that Mussolini used this newspaper to write anonymous articles to test the reaction of public opinion. When this became known, *Il Tevere* with its anti-Jewish diatribes was assumed to represent the current thinking of the Duce. It was true that Mussolini had made speeches linking Jewish financiers to Bolsheviks in Moscow and had spoken of them attempting 'to seek their revenge against the Aryan race' but this was probably no more than populist rhetoric, although these pronouncements were later presented as evidence that Italian anti-Semitism was not imported from Nazi Germany.[13] Apart from Aldo Finzi there were no Jews in the party hierarchy, but this scarcely suggests a deliberate policy of exclusion. Mussolini's mistress Margherita Sarfatti was Jewish, he appointed a Jewish minister of finance, Guido Jung (1932–35), and often requested the advice of Jewish experts and senators.[14]

On 14 July 1938 the appearance of the Manifesto of Racist Scientists, followed by a series of racial laws the following autumn and publicly defended by Mussolini on 18 September, took everyone by surprise. It was naturally assumed that this dramatic move was made in response to German pressure, that it was an integral part of the Axis, the close relationship established with the Reich since 1936 and perhaps the *sine qua non* of an even closer union. This was an important factor but there were other, equally significant reasons. *Romanità* had stressed race and much had been written and spoken about the Italic descendants of contemporary Italians. In the increasingly bitter attacks on the 'bourgeois mentality' culminating in Starace's anti-*lei* campaign of 1938, Jews were seen as embodying all the hated materialistic characteristics of the unheroic, grasping middle classes. With the growth of Zionism the creation of a Jewish state was seen as a threat to Italian interests in the eastern Mediterranean – 'another Gibraltar and Malta in *Mare Nostrum*' was the rather unrealistic complaint.[15] Zionists were also seen as subversives, living proof of the international Jewish conspiracy. Some Catholics were unhappy about a Jewish state in the Holy Land and there were some Jesuit writers in the *Civiltà Cattolica* who, living up to their reputation no doubt, made a fine distinction between ideological anti-semitism which was justified and Nazi racism which was not. This enabled Farinacci to reply to Pius XI's condemnation of racial theories (the pope followed up his encyclical *Mit Brennender Sorge* of 14 March 1937, which attacked Nazi racism, by deploring the racial laws in Italy) by saying 'we fascists can say concerning the Jewish question we have had as precursors the Fathers of the Company of Jesus'.[16] The Duce also angrily responded to papal strictures and the accusation that he was merely emulating the Germans (see Document 14). Yet another factor was the incessant demographic campaign, the battle of births which became obsessed by the 'defence of the race', in which racial purity began to be more important than sheer numbers. There were, therefore, within Italy and within fascism certain tendencies and developments which help to explain the events of 1938. Perhaps the most important of all the various explanations, however, is the impact of colonialism as a result of the conquest of Ethiopia in 1935.

It is certainly true that the annexation of territories inhabited by Germans in the South Tyrol, by Slavs in the region of Trieste and Fiume and by Arabs in Libya, had sharpened national awareness, leading to brutal programmes of italianisation;[17] but it was Italian contact with the black tribes of Ethiopia which provided the greatest stimulus for the growth of racial prejudice and, indeed, the 'imperial' necessity for it. Alarmed by rumours of intermingling between Italian troops and local inhabitants, Mussolini ordered a series of apartheid laws separating whites and blacks, with a five-year prison sentence for cohabitation. He insisted that a dominant race must behave with an aloof dignity, perhaps taking the British in India as his model. There was increasing emphasis on superior and inferior races and this naturally began to worry the Jews in Italy. Mussolini told the National Council of the party in October 1938 that the Italian inferiority complex must be overcome by the pursuit of harsh racial policies, and in Italy itself the Jews became the target.

After the Ethiopian campaign in 1936 Farinacci and Preziosi were not dissuaded from writing anti-semitic articles and in 1937 Paolo Orano, the writer and journalist, was commissioned to research and publish *The Jews in Italy*, which gave warnings of Anglo-Zionist collaboration against Italy and pointed to the sinister role played by French Jews in the Popular Front governments. This was still basically *political* anti-semitism. After the great exhibition celebrating the birth of Augustus historians and archaeologists set about proving that Italians were descended from a pure, Italic race – that they were, in fact, Aryans. Their 'discoveries' were exhibited in the *Mostra della Razza* in April 1940. This dealt with pre-historical findings, the Etruscans and the Romans and their direct descendants, the modern Italians. Giacomo Acerbo underlined this by publishing *I Fondamenti della Dottrina della Razza* (the foundations of race doctrine). But this was still *political* and *historical* in approach. Alberto Luchini, in charge of the 'race department' of Minculpop, developed these theories and made sure that schools, universities and academies were made aware of this new orthodoxy.

What was new about the manifesto of July 1938 and the articles in Interlandi's *La Difesa della Razza* was the introduction of bio-logical 'evidence' in support of anti-Semitism. The so-called scientists who signed the Manifesto had proved that there were superior and inferior races and Italians belonged to the former and Jews to the latter. This brilliant piece of research, which was praised by Starace and the Duce, was meant to pave the way for the racial laws which were approved between September and November 1938. Foreign-born Jews granted citizenship since 1919 lost their right to reside in Italy. Jewish children were excluded from school and not allowed to mix with Aryans; Jewish communities *were* allowed to provide their own schools. Mixed marriages were forbidden and if converted Jews were married in church the state would declare this invalid. Jews were purged from the party, the civil service, the armed forces, the professions and all cultural establishments. No Jew was allowed an Aryan servant, or to own a large business or a large estate. The definition of a Jew was not as rigorous as in the Third Reich and there were numerous exemptions for war veterans and their families, for those who joined the PNF in the early days and so on, but bureaucratic bungling and corruption often meant that these distinctions were not recognised and that pensions were not paid. During the summer and autumn of 1938 the entire Jewish community was in a state of deep shock.[18] So were some of the Fascist leaders. Among those who disapproved of the Law for the Defence of the Race were Balbo, who had close links with the Jewish community in Ferrara, De Bono, Federzoni, Gentile and Marinetti. Bottai was unhappy but he was under attack from

Interlandi and Giorgio Almirante (who became a post-war neo-Fascist leader) for his support for degenerate Jewish art and it was being whispered that his mother was Jewish.[19] Bottai gave way, remained education minister and implemented the racial laws in the state schools. Most Italians deplored this discrimination but there were no strong objections and gradually they seem to have accepted the situation. The church objected to the racial laws and for the first time since 1931 there was serious tension with the state. In general the pope condemned doctrines of inequality as unchristian, and in particular he condemned the banning of mixed marriages. He accused Mussolini of breaking the Concordat and he ridiculed him for copying the Germans and for misunderstanding the true nature of the Roman Empire – both points were calculated to enrage the Duce and they did (see Document 14). Mussolini had once noted that Suetonius refers to Jews standing guard over the tomb of Julius Caesar out of respect for his religious tolerance. To be reminded of his earlier interpretation of *romanità* was infuriating for the man who was always right – or so the slogan said. The physicist Enrico Fermi, winner of the Nobel Prize, left Italy, although he was non-Jewish, because he wished to show solidarity with his Jewish researchers. Margherita Sarfatti, former mistress of the Duce, was understandably distressed when her books were withdrawn from sale. Mussolini helped her to emigrate to Argentina in 1939. It was all a very sad commentary on a society that had prided itself on its humanitarian instincts. Indeed, these instincts were still alive and most Italians were prepared to help Jews in distress, including some officials charged with the implementation of the racial laws. It was only in 1943 when the Germans took over that extreme persecution began, with 9,000 Italian Jews transported to extermination camps. In retrospect, Mussolini realised he had made a great mistake but after the Pact of Steel and Italy's entry into the war alongside Germany he did not possess the courage to confess this publicly as it would seem to be a betrayal of fascist dynamism and – more importantly – it would alienate Hitler. Mussolini sought to reinvigorate the regime by his racial programme and his foreign policy. Both failed spectacularly, brought discredit upon Fascist Italy in general and on himself in particular. Racism and joining 'Hitler's war' were so unpopular that only victory could have saved the regime. But even an Axis victory would have left Italy a mere satellite of Nazi Germany.

Notes

1   G. Bonfanti, *Il Fascismo*, Brescia, 1976, ii, pp. 121–2.

2   *Ibid.*, p. 114.

3   A. Gramsci, *Letters from Prison*, London, 1979, pp. 42–5.

4   For this and other aspects of the regime see the invaluable P. Cannistraro, *La Fabbrica del Consenso: Fascismo e Mass Media*, Bari, 1975. Also P. Cannistraro, 'Mussolini's cultural revolution, fascist or nationalist?', *Journal of Contemporary History*, 7, 1972.

5   E. Gentile, *Il Culto del Littorio*, Bari, 1993, pp. 85, 87, 91.

6   E. Tannenbaum, *Fascism in Italy: Society and Culture 1922–45*, London,, 1973, p. 314.

7   R. Visser, 'Fascist doctrine and the cult of the Romanità', *Journal of Contemporary History*, 27, 1992.

8   *Ibid.*, p. 13.

9   M. Clark, *Modern Italy 1871–1982*, London, 1984, p. 244.

10   See Tannenbaum, *Fascism*, chs. 9–10.

11   'You cannot create fascism because of Mussolini' said Bottai; B. Guerri, *Giuseppe Bottai un fascista critico*, Milan, 1976, p. 202.

12   G. Bernardini, 'The origin and development of racial anti-semitism in Fascist Italy', *Journal of Modern History*, 1977, p. 439.

13   *Ibid.*, p. 435.

14   R. De Felice, *Mussolini il Duce*, Turin, 1981, II, p. 247.

15   Bernardini, 'The origin', p. 437.

16   *Ibid.*, p. 435.

17   See the excellent work by D. Rusinow, *Italy's Austrian Heritage*, Oxford, 1969.

18   A moving portrayal of Jewish families is in A. Stille, *Benevolence and Betrayal*, London, 1993. Also see J. Steinberg, *All or Nothing: The Axis and the Holocaust, 1941–43*, London, 1990.

19   Guerri, *Giuseppe Bottai*, p. 172.

6

Diplomacy, war and collapse

Foreign policy: the quiet years 1922–35

When Mussolini took over the foreign office in 1922 he moved it from the Consulta to new premises in the Palazzo Chigi. Those who imagined that this symbolised a completely new departure in Italian foreign policy were shown to be mistaken. Carlo Sforza, ambassador in Paris and former foreign minister under Giolitti, refused to serve the new government but there were few other serious defections. There was no systematic purge of personnel and attempts to bring in new blood in 1924 largely failed. Salvatore Contarini, the secretary-general of the foreign ministry, and his staff were prepared to work with Mussolini and he with them because they shared common aims. As staunch nationalists they supported the firm line adopted by the fascists towards the Germans, Croats and Slovenes in the newly annexed territories in the north; they too agreed that the 'Adriatic question' had not been fully resolved and that it might become necessary to exert pressure on the governments of Yugoslavia, Albania and Greece. Believing in Italy's imperial mission they sought spheres of influence and territorial gains in the eastern Mediterranean and Africa. Like Mussolini they felt humiliated by the condescending and sometimes contemptuous attitude of Italy's wartime allies, who were blamed for the 'mutilated victory'. Their attitude towards Mussolini and the 'fascist style' was ambivalent. They welcomed strong leadership and the promise of stability but they were apprehensive about Mussolini's impetuosity and his tendency to view European diplomacy through the eyes of a newspaper editor. What they failed to realise – and this led to

Contarini's resignation in 1926 – was the extent to which Mussolini would use his own personal agents and intermediaries in the pursuit of foreign policy. Important initiatives were often taken without consultation with the foreign ministry or even without informing it at all. Ambassadors tended to be ignored if they tendered unwelcome advice, and were sometimes totally unaware that unofficial channels of communication had been opened up to deal with crucial issues.

Mussolini was foreign minister from 1922 to 1929, from 1932 to 1936 and from February 1943. Dino Grandi, under-secretary from 1925, held the post between 1929 and 1932; Galeazzo Ciano, the Duce's son-in-law, was foreign minister from 1936 to 1943 and claimed, in his usual boastful fashion, that it was he who finally 'fascistised' the foreign ministry.[1] There was some truth in the claim but it was quite clear that throughout the regime it was Mussolini who conducted the foreign policy of Fascist Italy, whether he was nominally in charge or not, and whether he was using the personnel of the Palazzo Chigi or not. It was equally clear that he firmly believed that his credibility as a great leader depended upon his ability to make Italy feared and respected. The main purpose of assuming control in 1922 and consolidating the regime was to construct a powerful nation whose greatness was acknowledged throughout the world. The main purpose of propaganda was to prepare Italians for this historic role. Fascism glorified war and violence (see Document 2). As Social Darwinists Fascists believed in perpetual struggle and the survival of the fittest, convinced that 'youthful nations' like Italy were destined to overcome and supplant decadent states like France and Britain. Mussolini never tired of repeating that Italy must become a society permanently mobilised for war, that Italians must become more ruthless and militant. This ambitious programme was, of course, easier to enunciate than to fulfil. Mussolini had accepted Corradini's definition of Italy as a 'proletarian nation' (see Document 5). She was poised to inherit the wealth and the colonies of the plutocratic democracies but this did involve the realisation that Italy was *poor*. Deficient in vital raw materials, she had to import coal, iron and oil. More remarkably she was not self-sufficient in agricultural products, hence the 'battle for wheat'. There were always problems in balancing the budget and resolving currency difficulties, hence the 'battle of the lira'. Lack of capital resources hindered the rapid modernisation of plant in the factories and on the farms and imposed economies on the armed forces – a dangerous development for a regime with warlike intentions. A charismatic leader, a dynamic ideology and a well-organised propaganda machine might, just conceivably, conceal these weaknesses by a mixture of outrageous bluff and adroit diplomacy. It was a tremendous gamble which paid off for a decade and a half. So much depended upon the avoidance of false moves in the conduct of foreign policy.

Raffaele Guariglia, a career diplomat who served every government from 1909 to 1946, regarded himself as an expert in the theory and practice of Italian diplomacy. It would, he thought, be unwise to abandon the traditional policy of balancing one adversary against another and relying upon British support in times of crisis.[2] He upheld the old adage that whereas governments and regimes may change national interests remain the same. These interests were, to a large extent, determined by geographical position. Italy was clearly a Mediterranean power, with a long coastline, two large offshore islands and colonial possessions in Africa; she also controlled Rhodes and the Dodecanese islands in the Aegean. But Italy was also a continental power, the neighbour of France in the north-west and of the Germanic world beyond the Brenner. Additionally, because of the acquisition of Trieste and Istria, of Fiume (in 1924) and Zara, together with a near protectorate over Albania, Italy was the dominant power in the Adriatic and therefore closely involved in Balkan affairs. As a Mediterranean power she required a strong navy; as a continental power she required a strong army. A powerful air force would enable her to control the central Mediterranean area and win the respect of all her neighbours. For a country with limited resources this was too ambitious. To be effective Italy woud have to decide where her priorities lay. Only then could a realistic foreign policy be pursued and an appropriate strategy be devised by the armed forces. Confronted by a variety of possible alternatives, diplomatic and military, it was essential for the government to choose with care the policy and strategy to be adopted.

All post-war Italian governments had to decide whether or not to accept the 1919 Versailles settlement. Nationalist and Fascist attacks on the 'mutilated victory' made it difficult for Italy under

103

Mussolini to emerge as a satisfied, status quo power. Revision of the treaties was firmly on the agenda and yet it was realised, in private at least, that they offered Italy more security than she had ever enjoyed in the past. The acquisition of South Tyrol and the Trentino, the Brenner frontier and the seaport of Trieste strengthened Italy's position in the north and presented opportunities for further expansion in central and eastern Europe. The creation of an independent Austrian republic forbidden to join the rest of Germany was an additional safeguard. The collapse of the Habsburg Empire removed a formidable great power from the borders of Italy. The emergence of Yugoslavia prevented Italy from annexing large tracts of the Dalmatian coast, as promised in the Treaty of London of 1915, but the new state was divided and unstable and posed no serious threat. Some form of accommodation based on friendship or antagonism could surely be found. Italy was allowed a virtual protectorate over Albania and her relationship with Greece would depend on whether she had to surrender the Dodecanese islands to Athens or, as seemed likely, retain them. Spheres of influence in Anatolia and significant colonial adjustments appeared less capable of realisation. Overall, however, the post-war settlement left Italy in a very favourable position. The problem was that most Italians refused to draw this conclusion.

Mussolini was not alone in complaining that Italy had become a prisoner in the Mediterranean (see Document 15). It was easy to see why. Britain held Gibraltar, the islands of Malta and Cyprus, and controlled the Suez canal, with bases in Egypt and the mandate of Palestine. France, apart form her southern coastline, which included the port of Toulon, held Corsica, Morocco, Algeria, Tunisia with its naval base at Bizerta, and the mandates of Lebanon and Syria. The combined fleets of Britain and France dominated the Mediterranean and their garrisons in Egypt and Tunisia held the Italian colony of Libya in a vice. Cautious realists like Contarini and Guariglia advocated friendly relations with these wartime allies, but Mussolini resented their dominance and felt that Italy could only become a truly independent great power by 'breaking the chains' and 'marching towards the oceans'. Fascist rhetoric continued to attack the decadent democracies for their behaviour past and present and looked forward to their inevitable collapse. France, in particular, was subjected to continuous criticism. There were several reasons for this. Anti-fascists forced into exile settled in Paris and were allowed to conduct their political activities and publish newspapers hostile to the regime. There was still the unresolved problem of the status of Italians living in Tunisia. Another area of disagreement arose over the French diplomatic offensive in eastern Europe – the signing of treaties with Poland and with the Little Entente states of Czechoslovakia, Romania and Yugoslavia. Franco-Italian competition in eastern Europe helped to propel Mussolini to adopt a hard line towards Yugoslavia and closer links with revisionist powers like Hungary and Austria.

Between 1922 and 1935, however, Mussolini did not have much room for manoeuvre. These were comparatively 'quiet years', not because Mussolini had abandoned bellicose attitudes for respectable statesmanship but because suitable opportunities for a more forward policy did nto present themselves and because domestic issues required close attention. There was, nevertheless, one noisy episode which seemed to suggest that a new style of Fascist diplomacy really did exist, and was some-thing more than mere rhetoric. This was the Corfu incident of 1923.[3] At the end of August four Italians were murdered on Greek territory. They were working for the League of Nations boundary commission along the Greek/Albanian border. Mussolini, who was expecting Greek protests over the transfer of the Dodecanese to Italy, seized on this pretext for exerting pressure on Athens. Ships and men were *already* asembling in the area so this atrocity was well timed. An ultimatum was sent to the Greek government, which disclaimed responsibility for the mur-ders and so Italy bombarded and occupied Corfu, a strategically located island at the entrance to the Adriatic.[4] Greece appealed to the League but the French – engaged in an occupation of their own in the Ruhr – succeeded in referring the matter to the conference of ambassadors. Greece was forced to pay compensa-tion and pressure from the British induced the Italians to evacu-ate Corfu on 27 September 1923. Mussolini, who probably hoped to annex the island, claimed a great victory and his opponents rejoiced at his defeat. Calling this affair a dress rehearsal for the defiance of the League over Ethiopia in 1935 or for the invasion of Greece in October 1940 seems rather far-fetched. International alarm soon died away and there was general relief when Italy signed an agreement with Yugoslavia in January 1924 and peacefully acquired sovereignty over Fiume. This was followed in 1925 by Mussolini's grudging consent to join Britain as a co-guarantor of the Locarno Pact, which stabilised the Franco-German and German-Belgian borders. The opportunity to guarantee the Brenner frontier was missed. but the participation of Italy in the Locarno Pact suggested that Mussolini was prepared to play a responsible role in European diplomacy.

Dino Grandi, appointed undersecretary in the foreign ministry in 1925, had helped to persuade Mussolini to accept Locarno and to listen to the advice of those who argued that *Realpolitik* (a realistic policy based on facts and the balance of forces) was more appropriate than a policy based on ideological considerations (see Document 10). Since his days as a *squadrista* Grandi had changed dramatically and become much more conservative, finding more common ground with men like Federzoni (whom he served as undersecretary of the interior) or Contarini (who welcomed his appointment to the foreign ministry) than with most of the Fascist leaders, perhaps Mussolini included. It was assumed that Grandi would fascistise the foreign ministry, but he rapidly came to accept the views and the expertise of the career diplomats. For instance, he disciplined the *fasci all'estero* (there were around 600 *fasci* in foreign countries by 1930), who were creating problems for Italian ambassadors and consuls by engaging in political activities and disseminating Fascist propaganda. They were brought under strict control and ordered to concentrate on cultural activities. Grandi was keen to emphasise the non-ideological nature of Italian foreign policy: 'Fascism is not – and Mussolini has said this repeatedly – an article for export, nor has it ever claimed to be a universal idea or ideology' (this is in Document 10). Being able to quote the Duce greatly strengthened his hand. In Mussolini's first great 'changing of the guard' in 1929 (there were other reshuffles in 1932, 1936, 1939 and 1943) Grandi was promoted to the rank of foreign minister, the post held, of course, by Mussolini himself since 1922. He was convinced that Italy must avoid involvement in any major European war, that French hegemony must be ended and that Italian imperial ambitions in Africa could be realised without any great power conflict. To achieve these aims he was prepared to use the machinery of the League of Nations, to participate in disarmament conferences and to manoeuvre Italy into a position enabling her to become the 'determining weight' between Germany and France. Pointing to the fact that Italy had been among the first to recognise the Soviet Union in 1924, Grandi supported Russian entry into the League, but this and his growing anglophilia began to disturb Mussolini and the Fascist leadership. There seemed to be nothing even remotely 'Fascist' about his policies. The Duce, perhaps because he had now successfully concluded the Lateran Pacts with the universal church, began to speak of Fascism as a universal idea, 'Italian in its particular institutions, universal in spirit' (27 October 1930).[5] Soon he was proclaiming that 'the twentieth century will be the century of Fascism. Grandi's approach was no longer acceptable and the Duce took over the foreign ministry in 1932; he sent Grandi to London where he remained as ambassador until 1939.

The Duce's interest in 'universal fascism' lasted from 1930 to 1934.[6] He was influenced by his brother Arnaldo, who had edited *Il Popolo d'Italia* until just before his death in 1932. No one was closer to the Duce than Arnaldo, so his views were treated with great respect. He was arguing in favour of greater dynamism, of presenting the youth of Italy with a vibrant ideology and of promoting a cultural revolution. Bottai was writing in similar vein in his *Critica Fascista* and so was Gastone Spinetti, whose book *Fascismo Universale* was published in 1934. A journal entitled *Fascismo Universale* was founded by Asvero Gravelli on 28 October 1932 as part of the celebrations surrounding the Decennale. An international centre was established in Lausanne for the study of Fascism and various societies sprang up dedicating themselves to this new theme. Older societies, like the Dante Alighieri and even the *fasci all'estero*, were encouraged to publish pamphlets and hold conferences – Fascism was now emphatically for export. The climax – or rather the anticlimax – came with the Montreux congress in December 1934. Thirteen countries were represented but there was one highly significant absentee. The new Nazi Germany boycotted the meeting. There soon emerged serious disagreements among the delegates, especially over the Jewish question, and the establishment of a Fascist International was something of a mockery. It was agreed that all Fascisms had nationalism as their core but it was hoped that hostility to Marxism and capitalist egoism, together with support for corporativism and 'the idea of youth', would be sufficient to produce coherence! A permanent commission was set up to exchange ideas and propaganda but it ceased to meet after April 1935. By then the whole idea had become an embarrassment to Mussolini and Ciano. There were more urgent matters requiring attention.

At first the Duce found it difficult to assess the true significance of Hitler's triumph in January 1933. In his writings and speeches the Nazi leader had praised Mussolini and had posed as his disciple; he had underlined Germany's need to co-operate with Fascist Italy. This was all very reassuring and Mussolini undoubtedly felt flattered. But Hitler's rapid consolidation of power within the Third Reich created certain misgivings. With her vast potential, Germany was unlikely to remain a junior partner for very long and Berlin would soon rival Rome as the Mecca for fascists. As an Austrian who only secured German nationality in 1932 and as the author of *Mein Kampf* it was clear that *Anschluss* (the union of Germany with Austria) was a top priority. Mussolini's attempt to insert Germany within a new diplomatic grouping – the Four Power Pact of Germany, Italy, France and Britain signed in the summer of 1933 – proved a grave disappointment. The granting of 'equality of rights' to Germany in the question of rearmament was the major stumbling block, and France amended the original draft in such a way that it became a virtually meaningless document. When Germany left the disarmament conference and the League in the autumn the failure of this enterprising initiative was complete.

The first meeting of the two dictators in Venice in June 1934 was not a success. The Duce found his German counterpart distinctly unimpressive and they agreed about nothing of significance. Both men were clearly unprepared to commit themselves to any common line of action and at least one of them was totally preoccupied by domestic problems – a few days after this meeting on 14 June Hitler eliminated the SA leadership in the infamous Night of the Long Knives. Mussolini had raised the question of Austria but received no satisfactory response. His inquiry was more than justified by the events of the next month.

On 25 July Chancellor Engelbert Dollfuss was assassinated by Austrian Nazis during an attempted coup. Mussolini regarded this as a personal insult – the murdered man's wife was a guest of the Duce at the time, and it was well known that Dollfuss and Mussolini had been staunch political allies for over two years. But it was also a serious threat to Italy's security. Since the late 1920s Mussolini had sent money and arms to Prince von Starhemberg's paramilitary organisation the Heimwehr, and when Dollfuss became chancellor in 1932 he sent advice as well: to preserve Austrian independence and ensure Italian protection the Vienna government must strike hard at its enemies and establish an authoritarian, corporativist state. Dollfuss agreed and the Communists and Nazis were outlawed in 1933, and the Social Democrats were smashed in the spring of 1934. Mussolini responded swiftly to the challenge of the Austrian Nazis, determined to prevent *Anschluss*. Troops were sent to the Brenner and warnings to Hitler. The German leader proclaimed his innocence and the coup failed. Mussolini's defence of the Versailles settlement was warmly applauded by the British and the French and Italo-German relations became tense.

For the first time since the war a Franco-Italian *rapprochement* became possible. It was true that the murder of King Alexander of Yugoslavia and Louis Bartou, the French foreign minister, led to some hesitation, as the assassins in Marseilles were Croatian terrorists believed to have been trained in Italy. However, Italian friendship was regarded as too valuable to be thrown away. In January 1935 the new French foreign minister Pierre Laval arrived in Rome to sort out various points of disagreement in Tunisia and elsewhere, to jointly guarantee the status quo in Austria and the Balkans, and to sanction Italian expansion in Ethiopia. When Hitler tore up the disarmament clauses of the Versailles treaty and introduced conscription in March 1935, Mussolini went in person to Stresa to meet with the British and French representatives. At the meeting in April they agreed to reprimand Germany for her unilateral denunciation of treaty obligations, and this so-called Stresa Front seemed to align Italy with the democratic powers of the West against German expansionism. Britain and France remained silent over possible Italian expansionism in Africa. Franco-Italian relations had improved to such an extent that in the summer of 1935 General Pietro Badoglio and his general staff met with their French counterparts to plan for joint action against Germany on the Rhine and on the Brenner. Foreign policy and military planning began to consume the energies of Mussolini and the Fascist leadership. 'Better to live one day as a lion than a thousand years as a sheep' became one of the slogans. The quiet years were over.

Ethiopia

Although it need not have been so, the colonial war in Ethiopia proved to be the crucial turning-point in the history of the Fascist regime and in the diplomatic history of inter-war Europe. It was an excessively well-planned operation, the preparations for it were extravagantly advertised and – after a faltering start – it was effectively executed. In the short term it mobilised the Italian nation, enhanced the prestige of the regime and raised the cult of the Duce to dizzying heights. Yet in less than ten years his corpse was hanging upside down in the Piazzale Loreto in Milan, being reviled by an angry mob. Reading Gustave Le Bon had shown him the volatility of crowds but perhaps Mussolini had not anticipated such a macabre descent from glory (see Document 1).

The first attempt by Italy to advance into the highlands of Ethiopia from their colony in Eritrea had met with bloody defeat at the battle of Adowa in 1896. Nationalists had clamoured for revenge ever since. Mussolini agreed with them but in the 1920s there were other priorities, which included the reconquest of Libya through a brutal campaign of repression by General Rodolfo Graziani, successfully completed only in 1932.[7] It was in this year of the Decennale that the Duce began to plan the invasion of Ethiopia.[8] The pretext for the war came in December 1934 with a frontier skirmish at Wal Wal, an oasis on the borders of Italian Somaliland. Italy strenuously resisted all attempts at mediation inside or outside the League of Nations. Ethiopia had been admitted to the League and the Emperor Haile Selassie naturally sought its protection if the dispute could not be resolved in any other way. With military preparations well in hand, Mussolini was convinced that Britain and France would have no serious objections. Their colonies bordered on Ethiopia, and a series of agreements dating back to 1906 and renewed in 1925 had recognised it as an Italian sphere of influence. This also seemed to be the message brought by Laval in January 1935 and silently sanctioned by Britain and France in April at the Stresa meeting. In addition, Mussolini obtained a copy of the Maffey

Report on British interests in Ethiopia. Its conclusions, drawn up in June and accepted by the Cabinet in August, stated: 'No vital British interests exist in Ethiopia or in adjoining countries sufficient to oblige His Majesty's Government to resist a conquest of Ethiopia by Italy.'[9] This British attitude seemed to be confirmed when the League of Nations minister Anthony Eden went to Rome on 24 June to present Mussolini with a plan to allocate the Ogaden region of Ethiopia to Italy, and to compensate the emperor by granting him access to the sea – the so-called 'corridor for camels' – by the British cession of their port of Zeila. The plan was rejected and Eden never forgave Mussolini for this. It had shown, however, that the British government was prepared to dismember Ethiopia. This was welcome news for the Duce.

What Mussolini and, indeed, the Baldwin Cabinet had failed to appreciate was the growing strength of pro-League sentiment among the electorate. Public opinion can, of course, be manipulated or ignored but the imminence of elections does tend to concentrate the minds of governments and members of parliament, and elections were due to be held in November in Britain and in April 1936 in France. The results of the Peace Ballot sponsored by the League of Nations Union were published in London on 27 June 1935. They showed remarkable support for sanctions against an aggressor, and Italy had made no secret of her intention to become one if necessary. Because of the prolonged nature of the dispute there had been time for sympathy for Ethiopia to grow stronger. This was increasingly apparent and it prompted the foreign secretary Sir Samuel Hoare to make his famous speech at Geneva, when he pledged British support for League action against aggressors. It has been shrewdly observed that Hoare's speech of 11 September was as much a challenge to Prime Minister Laval as to Mussolini.[10] The smaller members of the League were anxious to follow the lead given by Britain and this put pressure on Laval to support her. France was nevertheless unwilling to sacrifice her military agreement with Italy, and feared that sanctions might lead to war. With the British Home Fleet steaming towards Gibraltar, the admiralty requested French co-operation in the Mediterranean and the right to use the naval facilities at Toulon and Bizerta. Laval was reluctant to comply. He realised, however, that if he had to choose between Italy and Britain he would have to choose the latter. There was some consolation in the knowledge that Britain was opposed to military sanctions and that everything possible would be done to avoid a direct confrontation. The League's condemnation of Italy if she became the aggressor did not imply an Anglo-French war against Italy. Mussolini was aware of this, of the doubts and hesitations of the two democracies and also, it seems, of the shortage of ammunition on British warships.

Month after month troopships had sailed from Naples to the Red Sea via the Suez Canal. This was no secret operation and by September 1935 there was no turning back for Mussolini. Badoglio and the military, the officials at the Palazzo Chigi and dozens of foreign governments had urged him to accept a compromise solution and thus prevent the possibility of war. They were contemptuously ignored. His propaganda machine was working as never before, the church supported his civilising mission, the party and the youth of Italy were enthusiastic, the women of Italy were prepared to donate their wedding rings and even the king looked less pessimistic. It was, therefore, with great confidence that he stepped out onto the balcony of the Palazzo Venezia to deliver his defiant decision for war and to issue his challenge to the League of Nations. On the following day, 3 October 1935, the invasion of Ethiopia began. Italy neglected to denounce the Treaty of Friendship signed in 1928 or even to declare war.

In these circumstances the League's condemnation of Italy as an aggressor was a foregone conclusion and this duly took place on 7 October. The debate over economic sanctions took longer. The decision to exempt oil was taken because Mussolini had made it clear he would regard that as an act of war. In any case, Germany, Japan and the United States were all non-League members prepared to export forbidden items to Italy. Britain opposed the closure of the Suez Canal. The imposition of sanctions, however feeble, enabled the Duce to claim that he was not only fighting the Ethiopians but fifty nations who had supported the punitive moves. Hatred of Britain and France, who were the ringleaders, grew alarmingly in some Fascist circles. The anglophobic D'Annunzio 're-discovered' the greatness of Mussolini and gave his wholehearted support.[11] It was this 'cold war' with the democracies that united the Italians behind their leader.

The democracies were increasingly uncomfortable and wished to bring the war to an end – if possible before it had really begun. With the November elections behind it Baldwin's National Government took a more cavalier attitude towards public opinion. Together with ambassador Grandi, Sir Robert Vansittart (permanent undersecretary at the Foreign Office) and foreign secretary Hoare drew up a plan for the partition of Ethiopia which the cabinet accepted. One 7 December 1935 Hoare met with Laval in Paris and devised a compromise scheme which was less generous to Italy. Mussolini was tempted, as the campaign in Africa was not going well, but this Hoare-Laval Plan was torpedoed when it was prematurely leaked to the press. An outraged public opinion in Britain forced the cabinet to disown the plan on 18 December and to offer up Hoare as a scapegoat. Hoare was replaced by Eden, a move which displeased the Duce. Laval fell in January 1936, but largely because of economic problems. Eden began pressing for oil sanctions but Hitler's remilitarisation of the Rhineland on 7 March 1936 created a massive diversion. Britain and France now had to consider the implications of a move which threatened to destroy the entire security system for Europe established at Versailles and Locarno. The Hoare-Laval Plan and the Rhineland crisis preserved Mussolini from undue interference. His armies, now commanded by Badoglio, pushed forward with greater speed and on 5 May 1936 Addis Ababa, the emperor's capital, was taken. On 9 May the Duce made another speech from his balcony announcing complete victory and the king's assumption of the title of Emperor of Ethiopia. After fifteen centuries, he roared, there was again a Roman Empire.

This war was the most popular in the history of modern Italy. Nearly half a million men, equipped with modern weapons, aircraft and poison gas had defeated the enemy in less than nine months, with only negligible casualties. The Italians had defied the world. Their leader had confirmed the truth of the writing on the wall proclaiming 'Mussolini is always right'. Despite Badoglio, the king, and the diplomats Mussolini had pressed ahead with his campaign and proved them all wrong. In another sense, however, the writing was on the wall.

The euphoria of 1935–36, partly manufactured and partly genuine, was short-lived. The problem with euphoria is that it is difficult to sustain and once dissipated leaves behind a sense of disillusionment and anticlimax. To prevent this Starace undertook various curious initiatives, and Mussolini and Ciano believed that a dynamic foreign policy would maintain the momentum. These efforts proved to be counter-productive. The increased emphasis on racism was a product of the Ethiopian war, evolving from the problems of white-black relations rather than the presence of the Jewish *falasha* (this community that was airlifted to Israel in recent years) in that part of Africa. There were many other serious consequences which need recording. Mussolini became over-confident, scornful of the advice proffered by professional soldiers and diplomats, and too prone to believe his own propaganda. The war had been very expensive and there had been a high wastage, not of men but of weapons and transport; nor had the campaign ended in 1936 – there was almost continuous guerrilla warfare until the British liberated the country in 1941, and this was a heavy burden for a faltering economy and an overstretched military establishment. Ethiopia, because of its geographical position, was difficult to defend and became a kind of hostage. Mussolini's African adventure also led to the grandiose schemes for marching to the oceans – from Libya and through the Sudan and Ethiopia to the Red Sea and the Indian Ocean or from Libya westwards through French and British territories to the Atlantic (see Document 15). States trapped within an inland sea, the Duce said, could only be semi-independent. This concentration on breaking out of the Mediterranean not only meant confrontation with the western democracies but also the abandonment of other spheres of influence. Mussolini had intended to conduct a swift campaign while Germany was still in the initial stages of rearmament, and then return to Europe to defend Austria and the Balkans. After Hitler's move into the Rhineland and the implications this had for *eastern* Europe (with France less able to assist the Little Entente), Mussolini realised he could no longer act as the protector of Austria and had to accept the Austro-German agreement of July 1936, which was an obvious prelude to the *Anschluss* of March 1938.

The League of Nations boycott, which was ended in July 1936 – enabling the Duce to claim victory over fifty nations – had intensified the drive towards autarchy. Import controls, exchange control, the search for ersatz materials such as a substitute for rubber, and increasing state intervention in industry, with IRI playing a major role, were never likely to create a self-sufficient Italy. Economically, Italy could not stand alone – her African colonies were a drain on her limited resources rather than valuable assets. Politically, Italy could not stand alone – unless she chose to become a second-rate power. This would be intolerable for the new Roman Empire, so Mussolini in 1936 had basically three choices: he could try to act as mediator between Germany and the western democracies, he could rejoin the British and French in a revived Stresa Front, or he could align himself with the Third Reich. The impact of the Ethiopian war made the last alternative seem the most attractive.

The Axis

Mussolini announced the existence of a Rome-Berlin Axis during a speech in Milan on 1 November 1936. His son-in-law Ciano, foreign minister since the previous June, had just visited Germany for talks with foreign minister Baron von Neurath and Hitler. Agreement had been reached over various issues and formed the substance of the October Protocols.[12] It was this *rapprochement* with Germany which Mussolini called the Axis. It was not a treaty or an alliance, but the name stuck and became the symbol of a close partnership. Ciano's negotiations laid the foundations for this. Germany recognised the new Italian Empire and Italy acknowledged German predominance in Austria. That removed two barriers. Both countries agreed to keep a close watch on British plans of encirclement, although Ciano shrewdly observed that Hitler's attitude to Britain was ambivalent. There was complete agreement over the Communist threat and Neurath informed Ciano of the negotiations with Japan, which resulted in the signing of the Anti-Comintern Pact on 25 November; Italy joined it a year later. The intelligence services of the two regimes had, in fact, already begun to co-operate; in September 1935 Admiral Canaris, head of the armed services intelligence, had met his counterpart General Roatta to exchange information and in March 1936 Himmler and Bocchini signed an agreement in Rome. Mussolini dated the birth of the Axis to September 1935 at his meeting with Hitler exactly two years later.[13] Finally, they agreed to collaborate even more closely in the Spanish civil war and to recognise the authority of General Francisco Franco.

When the civil war broke out in July 1936 Mussolini, after some hesitation, decided to respond to Franco's appeal for aircraft. Franco needed to cross over from Morocco to the mainland to assist the other Nationalist forces rebelling against the Republican government in Madrid. The Spanish military and some monarchists had been in contact with Rome on two occasions, in 1932 and 1934, but Italy had played no part in the attempted coup in July. Mussolini's decision to intervene and eventually to send over 50,000 'volunteers' and massive quantities of aircraft, arms and transport, was prompted by several considerations. In Februrary 1936 a Popular Front government, supported by Socialists and other left-wing elements, had taken office after the electoral defeat of the conservatives who had run Spain since 1933. This was alarming enough, but when a Popular Front government under the Socialist Léon Blum also assumed power in France Mussolini became decidedly apprehensive. When Franco and the generals rose up against the Republican government Mussolini was convinced that Blum would intervene to crush the revolt. It was this prospect which led him to proffer aid to the rebels. For domestic and diplomatic reasons Blum did not order the French army across the Pyrenees, but the Duce was already committed. Hitler had also decided to intervene and it was soon apparent that the Soviet Union was aiding the Republic, so these were two additional reasons for remaining involved in what was evolving into a bitter civil war. Franco, Salazar's Portugal, Nazi Germany and Fascist Italy combined to confront the Spanish Republicans, the International Brigades, the Socialists, the Communists, the Third International and Stalin's Russia. It could be seen as an ideological war between Fascism and Communism, being fought in Spain but having global implications. This was a gross over-simplification but the two dictators saw no reason to offer a more sophisticated version. Mussolini certainly had several practical objectives in mind. Securing a victory for Franco might entitle Italy to claim economic privileges and perhaps even naval bases in the Balearic Islands. The British might be forced to abandon Gibraltar, ending Anglo-French domination of the western Mediterranean. There were also sound domestic reasons for fighting in Spain. It would maintain the momentum achieved during the recently ended Ethiopian campaign, and it would certainly please the church, which saw the war as a crusade against the atheistic forces of Marxism and anarchism. It was yet another 'civilising mission'. Unfortunately for the Duce, the disadvantages of involvement outweighed the advantages.

The civil war lasted longer than Mussolini or anyone else expected. Franco's victorious entry into Madrid had to be postponed from the autumn of 1936 to the spring of 1939.[14] During this period the Italians lost over 4,000 men killed and many more injured. Hundreds of aircraft, tanks and guns were sent, together with thousands of military vehicles and rifles. Few of them were returned to Italy, where the government was slow to replace these losses and even slower to order newly designed weapons. The military and financial help for Franco cost 7,500 million lire and Italy received virtually nothing in return. Indeed, there was the humiliation of the defeat of Italian troops at Guadalajara in March 1937; what made it worse was the knowledge that anti-Fascist Italians fighting for the republic had helped to inflict this defeat. Opponents of the regime like Carlo Rosselli seized this opportunity to raise the morale of the anti-Fascists inside and outside Italy. 'Today in Spain, tomorrow in Italy' became an effective battle cry.[15] Three months later Rosselli and his brother were tracked down in France and assassinated. What his enemies called the 'Spanish Caporetto' forced Mussolini to reinforce his troops and keep them in Spain until they had won sufficient battles to wipe out the memory of Guadalajara.

Because of Italian intervention in Spain, with the flouting of the Non-Intervention Committee sponsored by Britain and France, and the submarine attacks on shipping in the western Mediterranean, it became increasingly difficult for the western democracies to resume friendly relations with Mussolini. Neville Chamberlain tried hard enough, seeking to rebuild an Anglo-Italian *entente* after he had become prime minister in May 1937. Those who stood in his way – Vansittart or foreign secretary Eden – were neutralised or forced to resign. Mussolini took his conciliatory attitude to be a sign of weakness and responded by acting even more outrageously, despite ambassador Grandi's advice. When the Duce visited Germany in September 1937 he found Nazi power a much more compelling argument; in November he joined the Anti-Comintern Pact and in December he withdrew from the League of Nations. Diplomatically and ideologically, the Duce appeared to have made his choice. He had turned his back on the democracies and opted for the Axis.

When Hitler made his long anticipated move and marched into Austria in March 1938 the Duce made no objections. 'Please tell Mussolini that I shall never forget him for this' was one of the few promises which the Führer actually kept. The *Anschluss* took the German frontier to the Brenner, encouraged the Germans in the South Tyrol (despite Hitler's constant reassurances that he had no intention of incorporating them into the Reich) and effectively excluded Italian influence from central and eastern Europe. This was the price which the Duce had to pay for membership of the Axis and for becoming too involved in Spain and the Mediterranean. The Italian role, as far as Hitler was concerned, was to distract the attention of Britain and France away from his own designs in eastern Europe.

The intervention in Spain had never been popular with the Italian people, especially as it seemed to lead to closer collaboration with Germany. The racial laws and the *passo romano* did more than symbolise the Italo-German *rapprochement*: they indicated subservience. Asserting Italy's great power status by humiliating the British and French was, ironically, converting her into the satellite of Nazi Germany. The Czech crisis of the summer and autumn of 1938 at least offered Mussolini the appearance of being independent. With Europe on the brink of war after Chamberlain's failure to reach an agreement at Berchtesgaden and Godesberg, the Duce welcomed the chance to emerge as a mediator. To the outside world it was Mussolini who had persuaded Hitler to meet with Chamberlain and French Prime Minister Daladier at Munich on 29 September 1938. He was in fact merely aiding and abetting the Nazi leader. It was, however, 'peace in our time' and the Duce had played his part, even if the script had been written in German. When the crowds applauded his achievement on his return he was, on the one hand, quite gratified but, on the other, bitterly conscious that sixteen years of Fascism had failed to produce a warlike nation. He determined to press on with the racial laws and to encourage Italian claims for the French territories of Nice, Corsica and Tunisia – 'spontaneously' demanded by an excited chamber of deputies on 30 November 1938. Chamberlain's visit to Rome in January achieved nothing, except to confirm Mussolini's low opinion of democratic leaders.

Hitler's swift annihilation of rump Czechoslovakia in March 1939 did, however, force the Duce to reconsider his position. His speech of 26 March offering negotiations with France if Daladier was prepared to make concessions may have been an attempt to counter-balance the growing power of Nazi Germany; in any event, Daladier rejected this approach on 29 March. Britain and France proceeded to guarantee Poland; Italy invaded Albania – an unnecessary move spearheaded by Ciano and his clique of adventurers but supported by Mussolini, who wished to prove that the Axis could also work to the advantage of Italy and perhaps to show France and Britain that Italy was still worth courting. Their response to this on 13 April was a guarantee to Greece and Romania. When the Anglo-Turkish agreement was signed on 12 May Mussolini became convinced of the truth of the Axis propagandists' claim that they were being encircled.

It is only against this background that Ciano and Mussolini's inept handling of the Italo-German talks leading to the Pact of Steel on 22 May can be fully explained. For over six months the Duce had resisted German offers of an alliance but on 6 May when Ribbentrop met Ciano in Milan he ordered his foreign minister to conclude one as rapidly as possible. This was done by adopting the German draft of a treaty which committed Italy to the support of Germany in the event of her involvement in a war. Article 3 stated that if 'one of them became involved in warlike complications with another Power or Powers, the other . . . would immediately come to its assistance as an ally and support it with all its military forces on land, at sea and in the air'.[16] Ciano emphasised that Italy would not be ready for war until 1943 and this was confirmed in General Ugo Cavallero's Memorandum (belatedly added to the Pact); the Duce made it clear that European war must not be allowed to interfere with his exhibition (EUR) in 1942 to celebrate the twentieth anniversary of the regime and to attract badly needed foreign currency. In defence of the Pact of Steel, it has been argued that Mussolini believed it would help him to control Hitler and prevent the outbreak of war for three or four years; it would also deter the British and French from any more forward moves in the Mediterranean.[17]

Hitler went ahead with claims against Poland and had no intention of allowing Italy to interfere with his foreign policy. This was made brutally clear in August on two occasions. On the first, when Ciano went to Salzburg to warn Ribbentrop against war with Poland, he found the Germans preparing an imminent offensive. 'I return to Rome', wrote Ciano in his diary for 13 August, 'completely disgusted with the Germans, with their leaders, with their way of doing things. They have betrayed us and lied to us'.[18] Ciano records another shock in his diary for 22 August: 'Von Ribbentrop telephoned that he would prefer to see me at Innsbruck rather than at the frontier, because he was to leave later for Moscow to sign a political pact with the Soviet Union'.[19] The Nazi-Soviet Pact of 23 August took everyone by surprise. Catholics, conservatives and Fascists who believed that anti-Communism was the very core of their ideology, were stunned by the news (anti-Fascist Communists were even more bewildered). It helped Ciano to convince the Duce that Italy must remain neutral in the event of war. On 26 August Ciano and the chiefs of staff sent to Berlin a list of the raw materials and military equipment needed by Italy before she could enter the war. Ambassador Bernardo Attolico, on his own authority, informed the Germans that Italy required immediate delivery of the 17 million tons of raw materials and 17,000 vehicles which had been requested. Hitler realised that this indicated that Italy would not join Germany in the war; he accepted this but hoped that Italy would help to tie down the British and French if they fulfilled their guarentee to Poland.

With the German invasion of Poland just hours away, Ciano and Mussolini attempted another Munich, calling for a conference on 5 September. Hitler attacked on 1 September, Britain and France resisted the temptation to negotiate unless Germany pulled her troops out of Poland, and declared war on 3 September. Italy remained neutral, or non-belligerent as Mussolini preferred to call it. It was a triumph for Ciano and the peace party, reinforced by Mussolini's penultimate 'changing of the guard' in October, when the more warlike ministers were dismissed and the chiefs of staff of the army and the airforce, General Alberto Pariani and General Giuseppe Valle, were replaced for 'deceiving' Mussolini and pretending that Italy was prepared for war. Starace was also dismissed and the secretary-ship of the PNF was given to Ettore Muti, who by chance had been Ciano's co-pilot during bomber raids over Ethiopia! The Duce was unhappy about this repetition of the Italian neutrality of 1914, fearful of being accused of betrayal by the Germans and of cowardice by the rest of the world. Over the next few months his moods alternated to such an extent that rumours spread that he had become mentally deranged or, so Bocchini thought, suffering once again from syphilis. The explanation is less drama-tic. After the rapid collapse of Poland there was the period known as the Phoney War, when neither side took the initiative on the western front. There was therefore no indication whether Ger-many or the western powers would win the war or, indeed, whether there would be a war at all. Italy's 'determining weight' had to be kept in reserve and in the meantime she could enjoy the economic and diplomatic advantages of remaining neutral. For Mussolini this was too reminiscent of the arguments of Giolitti in 1914–15, which he himself had savagely refuted during his inter-ventionist campaign. When Hitler launched his *blitzkrieg* in Scandinavia in April and then swept through the Low Countries into France defeating Holland, Belgium and France and driving the British off the continent, the Duce hesitated no longer. The war, it seemed, was virtually over, so Italy could safely join her triumphant ally and hope to share in the spoils of victory. As in 1915 the calculation that the war would soon be over proved to be incorrect, but unlike 1915 Italy in June 1940 chose the losing side.

War and defeat

It was on 28 May 1940 that Mussolini finally decided to enter the war. He gave chief of staff Badoglio only a few days to make the necessary preparations and announced his decision from the Palazzo Venezia on 10 June (see Document 16). The previous doubts of Ciano, the king and the chiefs of staff were temporarily banished by the prospect of profiting from the astounding Ger-man successes without actually having to fight a European war. Just over a week later the Duce ordered his troops across the Alpine border of France just as the new Pétain government had admitted defeat and was about to sign an armistice. It was an inglorious little campaign, but Mussolini had wanted a few thousand Italian casualties to reserve his place at the negotiating table. In fact, most of the Italian casualties were the result of frostbite and Mussolini's annexationist demands had to be postponed because Hitler did not want to force Vichy France to fight on; the armistice terms did not require France to hand over her fleet to the Axis nor to surrender any of her colonies. Mussolini decided not to press his claims. This combination of military ineffectiveness, diplomatic failure and subservience to Hitler were an inauspicious beginning. Unfortunately for the regime they set a pattern for the future.

Military weakness had been built into the regime from the very start. Despite all the rhetoric about a 'nation in arms', Mussolini was willing to pay the price demanded by the military leaders for their continuing support. Basically, this was to be left alone to run their own affairs. Diaz and the generals expected to be freed from interference by the PNF and to be reassured that the militia would not become an alternative 'people's army'. They agreed that financial constraints would require the government to reduce military expenditure and accepted the need for economies, provided they were not at the expense of the officer corps. The aim of most senior army and naval officers was to return to the traditional organisation and way of life they had enjoyed before 1915. The airforce, being only a decade old with its status as an independent service being recognised in 1923, had no such traditions; this was one reason why it could become the 'most fascist' of the armed forces. All three services were determined to fight their own corners when it came to the allocation of funds and resources. This phenomenon, common to all military establishments, led to an unwillingness to collaborate or to consider joint ventures. Inter-service co-operation leading to combined operations – so vital for a country intent upon reinforcing its position in the Mediterranean – was tenaciously reisted; the inter-service rivalry which replaced it helps to explain many of the military disasters between 1940 and 1943.

The last great public debate about such matters was during General Antonino di Giorgio's tenure of the war office from April 1924 to April 1925. He had radical plans for restructuring the army, which involved reducing its size and spending the savings made on new equipment and better training. Suspicious of any innovations, organisational or technological, the more conservative generals opposed this and convinced the Duce to replace him. General Roberto Bencivenga joined the controversy by advocating an 'every-ready' elite force of 150,000 men (like Charles de Gaulle's support for a *force de frappe* ten years later), but as a member of the Aventine Secession who later challenged Arnaldo Mussolini to a duel, his plan was rejected and he was placed *in confino* at Ponza for four years. General Asclepia Gandolfo's similar scheme, backed by an enlarged militia which he then commanded, suffered a similar fate.[20] The revolutionary theories of Giulio Douhet were also widely discussed at this time. He believed that an independent force of strategic bombers could fire-bomb and gas enemy cities into swift submission and that armies and navies had become anachronistic. This doctrine found acceptance among airforce officers, giving them a perfect reason for rejecting inter-service collaboration, but it was predictably denounced as the ravings of a madman by the other armed services.

Increased censorship after 1925 effectively ended these discussions in the press and in parliament. Mussolini became the minister in change of all three services from 1925 to 1929 and then again from 1933 to 1943. In 1925 he appointed Badoglio as army chief of staff and chief of the general staff; he held the former post only until 1927 but held the latter until December 1940. Badoglio as chief of the general staff made no serious attempt to co-ordinate the three services, nor did he try to pursue Di Giorgio's ambitious reforms. In 1926 he and Cavallero, undersecretary for war, reorganised the army on its old traditional basis.[21] Without relinquishing his post, Badoglio accepted the governorship of Libya from 1928 to 1933 and commanded the Italian armies in Ethiopia in 1935–36. It was obvious that Mussolini did not want him to become an effective chief of general staff as this might challenge his own authority. What he did want, however, was the support of Badoglio and his colleagues for his propaganda campaign to convince the world that Italy could summon up an army of 'eight million bayonets', that his airforce could 'blot out the sun' and that his navy could control the Mediterranean. In 1940, out of seventy-three divisions only nineteen were complete and fully equipped.[22] Although Balbo had raised the prestige of the airforce (as undersecretary 1926–29 and as minister of aviation

1929–33) by his dramatic flights across continents and oceans, the aircraft it possessed in 1940 were too few in numbers and too outdated to inspire excessive confidence. The navy was in better shape, but until 1936 had never contemplated the awesome task of taking on the British fleet. General Alberto Pariani, under-secretary for war from 1936 to 1939, proclaimed Italy's readiness for 'a lightning war' (*guerra di rapido corso* or *blitzkrieg* as the sceptical Germans would call it) but this was sheer propaganda. Badoglio had never been convinced that tanks were really essential and plans for motorisation proceeded very slowly; he was often not invited to discussions about mechanisation and did not seem unduly perturbed by this! Pariani's other 'innovation' was to reduce the number of regiments in each division from three to two, again without informing Badoglio.[23] This enabled the number of divisions to be increased and it was supposed to improve their mobility, but these 'hollow legions' had grave deficiencies which actual warfare swiftly revealed.

When General Carlo Favagrossa took over as commissary general for war production in August 1939 he was appalled at the situation. The losses incurred in Ethiopia and Spain had not been made good, the decision to replace Italy's vintage artillery (the best had been captured from the Austrians in 1918) had only just been taken, and of the 1,500 tanks which had been manufactured only seventy were of medium size – the rest were three-ton machines dismissed by the troops as 'sardine tins'.[24] Staff officers, including their chief, had ignored the lessons of Africa and Spain and failed to study the implications of German and Soviet peacetime manoeuvres. Most alarming of all was the inability of Italy's war industries to supply more than a fraction of the requirements of the armed forces. Urgently needed were more armoured cars, anti-tank weapons, anti-aircraft guns and the list could go on. Fuel and other basic raw materials were also desperately short. Even the brief campaign in Albania in April 1939 against a largely non-existent enemy had emphasised Italy's unpreparedness for war.

'In Fascist Italy', Mussolini told the senate in March 1938, 'the problem of unified command which torments other countries is resolved. Politico-strategic war objectives are drawn up by the Head of Government. Their implementation is entrusted to the chief of general staff . . . In Italy the war, as it was in Africa, will be directed under the orders of the king, by one man: the man who now speaks to you'.[25] For this man, who had given himself the title of First Marshal of the Empire and run the three service ministries since 1933, to accuse Pariani and Valle of deceiving him was quite preposterous. If he was genuinely ignorant of the true state of affairs he was unfit to lead his country. If he did know and had failed to rectify the situation he was equally culpable. But so were the generals and political leaders who hailed him as a military genius and propagated the myth of the Duce whose iron will was sufficient to overcome all obstacles. The test came after the fall of France, with the British decision to fight on in the air, on the sea and on the land.

Before Italy's entry into the war, Mussolini had determined to fight a 'parallel war' alongside Germany. This Mediterranean strategy, outlined in February 1939 (see Document 15) was reaffirmed in a memorandum to the king on 31 March 1940.[26] Mussolini, to whom the king had reluctantly and ambiguously delegated his military prerogatives on 1 June, now had to implement this strategy.[27] It was vital to consult with Badoglio and the chiefs of staff, Generl Ubaldo Soddu, Admiral Domenico Cavagnari and general Francesco Pricolo. Together they constituted the Supreme Command and their basic task was to devise a coherent strategy. For several months they found it peculiarly difficult to decide upon any specific plan of action, or indeed whether they really needed to take the initiative in any of the possible theatres of war. This was not through cowardice or a realistic appraisal of Italian weakness. There were two very important reasons for this hesitancy. They were faced with so many possibilities that reaching a consensus was extremely difficult and time-consuming. Under consideration were the following:

- an attack in the Balkans, which would prove to Hitler that Italy was still a continental power but which he might – and did – find inconvenient for strategic and economic reasons;
- the elimination of Britain's base in Malta, which would raise the problem of co-ordinating air and sea power and which Badoglio deemed unessential;
- an invasion of Egypt from Libya to secure the Suez Canal, but this involved logistical difficulties across the sea and across the desert;

- an attempt to neutralise Gibraltar, but that might require Franco's support;
- direct participation in the invasion of the British Isles if Germany agreed.

If Italy concentrated on just *one* of these objectives a successful outcome was distinctly possible, even with her limited resources. The second reason for the hesitation of the Supreme Command was the confident expectation that although Britain had not followed the French example she would soon be defeated and forced to surrender her assets, which Italy could snap up without having fought for them. Hitler's cancellation or at least postponement of Operation Sealion (for the amphibious attack on Britain) in the autumn of 1940 falsified this happy prediction.

By this time the Duce needed a success. 'Hitler's war' was not popular with Italians despite the efforts of the propaganda ministry. Fascists who supported the war and had believed the rhetoric of the regime were perplexed by the inactivity of their armed forces. Admittedly, the exhilarating victories of the *Wehrmacht* were a hard act to follow, but Italy's 'parallel war' had not even started. One and a half million troops and six hundred generals (but only two NCOs per company compared to the Germans' twenty) were waiting for orders, some impatiently, some apathetically.[28] As if to make up for lost time, the Duce ordered two offensives in the autumn of 1940. On 28 October Greece was invaded, the choice of date (anniversary of the March on Rome) being easier to understand than the choice of victim. Ciano and his clique were sure that bribery and intrigue would open the way for an easy victory but were soon to be proved wrong. Mussolini made his move largely because Hitler's troops had begun to move into Romania and he wished to preserve Italian influence in the Balkans. Greece had been guaranteed by Britain in April 1939, but the Greek war was as much anti-German as anti-British – strange behaviour for a leader who had just (27 September) signed a Three Power Pact of solidarity with Germany and Japan. The other offensive was ordered in North Africa, where Marshal Graziani was prodded into action against the British in Egypt but only covered the 60 miles from the Egyptian border to Sidi el Barrani, where he was rapidly overwhelmed by a series of British counter-offensives beginning in December 1940. Meanwhile the incompetent General Visconti Prasca was also being forced into an ignominious retreat by the Greek army, who drove the Italians back into Albania. An additional disaster wass the devastating attack on the Italian fleet at Taranto on 11–12 November 1940, which gave the British temporary control of the central Mediterranean. The 'parallel war' was over almost as soon as it had begun. The *Wehrmacht* moved into the Balkans, defeating the Greeks and their British allies and annihilating the Yugolsav army. Yugoslavia was partitioned and by courtesy of the Germans Italian troops of occupation were stationed from Slovenia in the north to Greece in the south. In this humiliating fashion the Italians secured control of the Adriatic. Even this was an illusion as German interests always had priority, and the Italian troops soon found themselves involved in a savage war against Tito's partisans. In North Africa the situation was transformed by the arrival of Rommel's *Afrika Korps*, and in the see-saw battles of the desert war which followed it was German armour and German tactics and strategy which dictated the course of the campaign. The arrival of the *Luftwaffe* in southern Italy and Sicily to counter British sea and air power was the final assertion of Germany's total control over the Axis war effort. Hitler, exasperated by Italian failures, remained loyal to the Duce and rebuked those Germans who complained that they would prefer to see Mussolini as an enemy rather than an ally.

Mussolini hoped to shield himself by removing Graziani and by making Badoglio the scapegoat for the recent disasters. It was clear, however, that his regime could only survive if Hitler won the war, and even the anti-Germans realised this. But it was equally clear that a victorious Germany would place Italy in a very subordinate position. Hitler's negotiations with Pétain and Franco had already alerted the Duce to the possibility that Italy might be treated as a power comparable to Vichy France or Spain. It was no longer a question of asserting equality with the Reich but of ensuring that Italy was recognised as the most important of the lesser powers. It was for this reason, rather than for ideological motives, that Mussolini promptly offered Italian support for the invasion of Russia after June 1941. Eventually there were 227,000 Italian troops fighting in Russia. Vehicles and other equipment were sent which were urgently needed on the Mediterranean front, but even so they proved totally inadequate.

Caught up in the battles around Stalingrad the Italian divisions were cut to pieces. Another 'short war' had turned out differently. Only 77,000 survived, leaving behind 90,000 dead and 60,000 prisoners. Polverelli's propaganda machine failed to acknowledge the return of the remnants of the expeditionary force in March 1943.

By this time, Fascist Italy had been at war with the United States for over a year. After the Japanese attack on Pearl Harbor on 7 December 1941 both Germany and Italy had declared war on America. Italy was now enmeshed in what had become the Second World War, with Japan and the Axis locked in mortal combat with the Grand Alliance of Britain, Russia and America. The turning-point in this war came a few months later in the autumn of 1942. On the Russian front the Red Army's counter-offensive north of Stalingrad began on 19 November. In North Africa General Bernard Montgomery launched his attack at El Alamein on 23 October and on 8 November Anglo-American landings (Operation Torch) in Morocco and Algeria trapped the Italo-German forces in an allied pincer grip. The Italians had lost their empire in east Africa back in the spring of 1941 and now they were expelled from Libya. The final surrender of the Axis forces in North America took place in Tunisia in May 1943. Churchill's success in securing President Roosevelt's approval for American involvement in the Mediterranean – against the advice of the US chiefs of staff – sealed the fate of Mussolini's Fascist Italy. The next allied objective was Sicily, and after the swift conquest of the island it seemed only logical, at least to Churchill, that mainland Italy should be invaded. The rewards would be the equally swift conquest of Italy up to the Alps through the 'soft underbelly of Europe' and the overthrow of Mussolini. The latter was achieved fifteen days after the first landings in Sicily on 9 July, but the former took twenty-one months of bitter fighting and civil war.

The coup of July 1943 and its consequences

After more than two and a half years of war there were increasing signs of popular discontent, culminating in the wave of strikes in the industrial cities of the north in March 1943. This unrest was economic and not political; the strikes were ended by the grant of wage increases. Starved of vital raw materials, the factories were unable to replenish the depleted stocks of weapons and vehicles required by the armed forces, let alone supply the demand for consumer goods. Shortage of coal and oil was bringing production to a standstill. Cars were replaced by bicycles and horses. But it was the shortage of food and the high prices charged whenever it became available that created the most distress. As the war drew closer incessant bombing lowered morale and led to widespread defeatism. News from the battle fronts brought by returning soldiers or heard on Radio London and Vatican Radio was in stark contrast to the optimistic reports of Pavolini and Polverelli from the progaganda ministry. Mussolini's response to all this was yet another 'changing of the guard', dispensing with ministers like Ciano, Grandi and Bottai, replacing his chief of general staff Cavallero and bringing in General Vittorio Ambrosio. Two months later, in April 1943, he dismissed the young but useless Aldo Vidussoni as party secretary for failing to prevent the March strikes and appointed the old *squadrista* Carlo Scorza. Just as sacking Badoglio and Admiral Cavagnari in December 1940 had failed to stem the series of military and naval disasters, so this drastic purge only increased the confusion and bitterness in the ranks of the political and military establishment. The discontented masses and the scattered groups of anti-Fascists did not, as yet, threaten the Duce's authority. Ex-ministers and indignant Fascist leaders did.

The invasion of Sicily, the first bombing of Rome and Mussolini's failure to inform Hitler of Italy's need for peace when they met at Feltre on 19 July, at last produced a movement to reduce the power of the Duce or even to remove him. There were two distinct groups among the Fascist leaders, both calling for a meeting of the Grand Council which had not met since 1939. Farinacci and Scorza wanted it to sanction closer co-operation with Germany and a more vigorous prosecution of the war. Grandi, Ciano and Bottai had other ideas. Grandi drew up a resolution which would declare their lack of confidence in the Duce's leadership and express their determination to resolve full powers to the king. Mussolini agreed to hold the meeting on 24 July and when Grandi informed him of the proposal he neither reacted nor took counter-measures. Nevertheless, Grandi arrived with grenades in his pocket just in case. The meeting dragged on until the early hours of the following morning when

Grandi's resolution was passed by nineteen votes to seven. Mussolini seemed listless but unconcerned. After all, the Grand Council was only an advisory body (see Document 17). The next day he worked in his office and reported to the king at 5 p.m. His account was cut short by Victor Emmanuel, who informed him that he was appointing Marshal Badoglio as the head of a new government. The astonished Duce left and was immediately arrested and whisked away to prison in an ambulance. Much of the preparation for this coup had been the work of the Duke d'Acquarone, the minister of the royal household, with the connivance of leaders in the army and the *carabinieri*. When the radio announced the news there was universal rejoicing and neither the party nor the militia made any attempt to challenge the king and Badoglio. In his proclamation late in the evening of 25 July Badoglio added, for the benefit of the Germans, 'the war continues'.

The Germans were not deceived and Badoglio had the difficult task of negotiating secretly with the allies to secure some form of armistice, which avoided the unconditional surrender they were demanding while at the same time preventing German reprisals against an unfaithful ally. He also had to make sure that the Duce was held in a secure prison and moved from place to place to avoid any attempt at rescue. There was also the problem of dealing both with the Fascists and with the newly emerging political parties. It was ony on 3 September that the so-called 'short armistice' was signed in Sicily (the longer, more explicitly harsh armistice was signed on 29 September), just as allied troops were crossing into Calabria. Badoglio was anxious to keep this secret until the government could be sure of Anglo-American protection, but General Eisenhower insisted upon a public announcement which was made on 8 September to coincide with the American landings at Salerno. The Germans, who had been infiltrating troops across the Brenner for some weeks, now moved swiftly to occupy as much of the peninsula as possible. They swooped on Rome and forced the king and Badoglio to flee to the allied lines in the south. The Italian armed forces were left with no precise instructions and the army disintegrated, a large number of units being taken prisoner.[29] In the confusion the Duce was rescued by the Germans and taken to Munich on 12 September. The twenty-year Fascist regime had ended. The short, tragic episode of the Italian Social Republic was about to begin.

After 8 September 1943 Italy was divided into three. There was the liberated area in the south under the king and Badoglio, which expanded as the allies advanced (Rome and Florence were taken in the summer of 1944); in the centre was the battle zone and the north was under German occupation. In the centre and particularly in the north resistance groups, controlled by Committees of National Liberation (CLNs), sprang up to fight the Germans and the Fascists who still supported Mussolini. This plunged Italy into the civil war which Federzoni had hoped to avoid by supporting Grandi's resolution at the Grand Council meeting on 25 July (see Document 17).

Hitler bullied Mussolini into returning to Italy to rally his supporters and assist in the defence of the rapidly shrinking New Order. On 13 October Victor Emmanuel and Badoglio were bullied by the allies into declaring war on Nazi Germany and into accepting the role of 'co-belligerents'. This was essentially the status of Mussolini in the north with ragard to the Germans. Neither side seemed prepared to describe the Italians as 'allies'. Neither side permitted Badoglio or Mussolini to act independently.

Under the close supervision of SS General Karl Wolff, the Duce was installed in Gargnano on Lake Garda. The foreign ministry was based in nearby Salò and Mussolini's regime is often referred to as the Republic of Salò. Other ministries were scattered in various towns from Brescia to Padua. The Duce established his Italian Social Republic and re-named his party the Fascist Republican Party. His betrayal by the king had, of course, revived his old republicanism. The desertion of the middle classes, the industrialists and the army had prompted his determination to try to win over the working classes by a programme of 'socialisation'. The almost total disintegration of the PNF and the militia after 25 July had been a devastating experience for him, and it now posed the difficult problem of securing recruits for his ministries, his new party, his police and security forces. German control of communications and transport, together with the obvious fact that a large area of Italy had become a battleground, were added complications. He did, however, have a small nucleus of supporters – as one journalist unkindly wrote 'after the storm all the corpses float to the surface'.[30] There was Pavolini, who was made secretary of the party, Guido Buffarini Guidi, who became interior minister, and Marshal Graziani, who struggled against German opposition to establish a viable army. Farinacci returned to his fief in Cremona, ran it on behalf of the Germans but remained aloof from the government. The anti-semitic Preziosi intrigued with and against everyone, hoping for the fulfilment of his dream, the complete extermination of the Jews. Renato Ricci, *squadrista* and former president of the *Balilla*, headed the militia (Republican National Guard as it became called). There was, in addition, a large reservoir of manpower consisting of half a million Italian prisoners of war and 300,000 labourers, but they were in the Reich and the Germans intended to keep them there and perhaps even to add to their number. By November 1943 the Duce had done his best to fill the administrative posts and build up the police and the militia, and felt that it was time to hold a party congress at Verona.

The Verona manifesto of 14 November 1943 was notable for its emphasis on socialisation and the collective interest. It reminded the Italian people of the social reforms of the regime, promised even more and urged them to fight the invasion of the 'Anglo-American plutocracies'.[31] A year later in his last public speech, which was possibly his best, Mussolini explained that the programme of republican Fascism 'is but the logical continuation of the programme of 1919 – of the achievements of the splendid years that took place between the announcement of the Labour Charter and the conquest of the empire'.[32] Although the new party boasted nearly half a million members, the attempts to return to the 'Fascism of the first hour' and to outbid the Marxists by his socialisation schemes were doomed to failure. The Germans opposed anything which might hinder war production, the northern industrialists were hostile and the workers were sceptical, responding by strike action and boycotting elections to factory committees. What *was* happening, in fact, was a return to the *squadrismo* of the 1920s, with Black Brigades and other formations attacking their old enemies, the socialists and Communists. The difference was that these enemies could now hit back. Well-armed, organised resistance groups answered reprisals with reprisals and were able to win control over large areas of the countryside. Moves to conscript men into the armed forces and forced labour in the Reich led thousands of them to join the partisan bands in the hills and forests.

Apart from its inability to preserve even the semblance of law and order, the republic had lost all credibility by its failure to prevent the Germans from taking over the South Tyrol, Trieste, Fiume and all the lands which once belonged to the Habsburg Monarchy. It was this humiliation which most exasperated the Duce; these territories had been Italy's reward for all her sacrifices in the First World War. In his two meetings with Hitler in 1944 the Duce failed to secure any redress of his grievances. Their last meeting was on the day of the attempted assassination of Hitler on 20 July, and Mussolini was quietly pleased that his powerful friend also had enemies within. As the Grand Alliance closed in, the two dictators convinced themselves that Germany's secret weapons – and Londoners found that they did exist, as flying bombs, VIs and VIIs, fell on them – could turn the tide of battle and that before long the western democracies would find themselves in conflict with the Soviet Union. The realists in London and Washington would surely see the advantages of a strong anti-Communist Germany and Italy. They did, but this came two years after the death of Hitler and Mussolini.

When the Duce returned to the shores of Lake Garda there were no plans to celebrate the first anniversary of the Italian Social Republic. Its only memorable achievement was not so much the Verona manifesto of November 1943, but the Verona trial and executions of January 1944. Never particularly vindictive, Mussolini had succumbed to the pressure of those who were. Many of the Fascists who had joined him demanded vengeance on the traitors who had voted against him at the Grand Council meeting on 25 July. Most of them had fled or were in hiding but there were two notable exceptions, the old *quadrumvir* De Bono, and Ciano, who had been flown back from Germany. The Nazis were delighted to send him as they regarded him as a traitor who had consistently undermined the Axis. Despite the pleas of his daughter Edda and her threats to use his son-in-law's diaries to expose the hollowness and duplicity of the Italo-German relationship, Mussolini allowed the trial and execution to go ahead. It was, he realised, a test of his determination to abandon the compromises of the past and of his loyalty to the Reich. The mockery of a trial and the gruesomely mismanaged execution of Ciano and the others was a deplorable episode and an additional burden for the Duce to bear.

Finding the claustrophobic life by Lake Garda increasingly unbearable, Mussolini decided to move down to Milan on 18 April 1945. It was where Fascism had begun on 23 March 1919 and where it was to end on 29 April 1945. The allies were now moving rapidly into the Po valley and, unknown to the Duce, SS General Wolff had entered into secret negotiations with Allen Dulles of the American Office of Strategic Services in Switzerland. Wolff sought a separate armistice with the western allies for all German troops operating in Italy.[33] Cardinal Schuster, the archbishop of Milan, was also keen to protect his city and bring an end to the fighting by persuading Mussolini not to attempt a last stand there or in the Valtelline, but to enter into talks with the leaders of the national liberation movement. The movement's headquarters were in Milan and they were busily preparing a national uprising to coincide with the advance of the allied armies. The cardinal hoped to involve the Germans in these talks, but they had other plans. On 25 April Mussolini agreed to meet the partisan leaders in the archbishop's palace. They demanded his unconditional surrender and he seemed inclined to accept, but Graziani intervened to announce that he had just heard the Germans were on the point of signing an armistice. Mussolini appeared astonished and left hurriedly, promising to give his reply within the hour. However, fearing treachery, he decided to leave with his followers for Como. Once there, he found the partisan rising was in full progress so on 27 April, together with his mistress Claretta Petacci, he joined a German anti-aircraft unit heading north. The column was soon stopped by partisans who agreed to let it pass if they could first search for Italians. Mussolini was discovered and he was led away. The following day, on orders from partisan headquarters in Milan, he and Claretta Petacci were shot and their bodies brought back to the city to be strung up in the Piazzale Loreto early in the morning of 29 April. It was not far from the Piazza San Sepolcro or the building which had housed the editorial office of *Il Popolo d'Italia*. Hitler committed suicide on 30 April and a few days later the war in Europe came to an end. The Fascist era was over. Fascism, in various forms, lived on.

Notes

1 F. Gilbert, 'Ciano and his ambassadors', in G. Craig and F. Gilbert (eds.), *The Diplomats 1919–1939*, Princeton, 1953, p. 512. In the same volume see H. Stuart Hughes, 'The early diplomacy of Italian fascism 1922–32', p. 210–33.

2 R. Guariglia, *Ricordi 1922–46*, Naples, 1950, p. 146.

3 This is covered in J. Barros, *The Corfu Incident of 1923*, Princeton, 1965. The best account in English of these years is still A. Cassels, *Mussolini's Early Diplomacy*, Princeton, 1970. See also Cassels, *Fascist Italy*, ch. 5.

4 C. Lowe and F. Marzari, *Italian Foreign Policy 1870–1940*, London, 1975, pp. 194–5.

5 B. Mussolini, *Scritti e discorsi*, ed. V. Piccoli, Rome, vii, p. 230.

6 See M. Ledeen, *Universal Fascism*, New York, 1972.

7 For an excellent study of Libya see C. Segre, *The Fourth Shore: The Italian Colonization of Libya*, Chicago, 1974.

8 The most detailed study is G. Rochat, *Militari e politici nella preparazione della campagna d'Etiopia: studio e documenti 1932–34*, Milan, 1971.

9 E. Robertson, *Mussolini as Empire Builder: Europe and Africa 1932–36*, London, 1977, p. 145.

10 *Ibid.*, p. 173.

11 R. De Felice, *D'Annunzio politico 1918–1938*, Bari, 1978, pp. 216–20.

12 E. Wiskemann, *The Rome-Berlin Axis*, London, 1966, pp. 89–92.

13 *Ibid.*, p. 70.

14 See J. Coverdale, *Italian Intervention in the Spanish Civil War*, Princeton, 1975.

15 The authoritative work remains C. Delzell, *Mussolini's Enemies: The Italian Anti-fascist Resistance*, Princeton, 1961.

16 Text in Delzell, *Mediterranean Fascism*, pp. 208–10.

17 R. De Felice, *Mussolini il Duce*, ii, pp. 624–5.

18 G. Ciano, *Ciano's Diary 1939–1943*, London, 1947, p. 125.

19 *Ibid.*, p. 131.

20 G. Rochat, *L'Esercito italiano da Vittorio Veneto a Mussolini*, Bari, 1967, pp. 226–7, 518–19.

21 For a biography see P. Pieri and G. Rochat, *Badoglio*, Turin, 1974.

22 G. Rochat and G. Massobrio, *Breve storia dell'esercito italiano dal 1861 al 1943*, Turin 1978, p. 224.

23 J. Whittam, 'The Italian general staff and the coming of the Second World War', in A. Preston (ed.), *General Staffs and Diplomacy before the Second World War*, London, 1978, pp. 92–3.

24 C. Favagrossa, *Perchè perdemmo la guerra: Mussolini e la produzione bellica*, Milan, 1946, p. 16.

25 G. Bianchi, *Perchè e come cadde il fascismo*, Milan, 1970, p. 13.

26 F. Deakin, *The Brutal Friendship*, London, 1966, p. 24.
27 M. Knox, *Mussolini Unleashed 1939–41*, Cambridge, 1986, pp. 104–5.
28 G. Bocca, *Storia d'Italia nella guerra fascista*, Bari, 1969, p. 103.
29 The navy, however, arrived safely in Malta.
30 F. Deakin, *The Last Days of Mussolini*, London, 1966, p. 117.
31 Delzell, *Mediterranean Fascism*, pp. 237–42.
32 *Ibid.*, p. 245.
33 Deakin, *Last Days*, p. 270.

Epilogue: the legacy

After the July coup in 1943 the Fascist regime and the PNF disintegrated. In April 1945 the Italian Social Republic and the Fascist Republican Party were totally smashed and this time the charismatic Fascist leader was killed, so there could be no question of a dramatic rescue and return as in September 1943. Many of the party notables had died (Bianchi in 1930, Forges Davanzati in 1936), been killed (Balbo was shot down by friendly fire over Tobruk in June 1940, Gentile was assassinated in April 1944), executed for opposing the Duce (Ciano and De Bono in Verona in January 1944), or hunted down and murdered by partisans (Farinacci, Starace, Pavolini and after a summary trial Buffarini-Guidi). Preziosi committed suicide, De Vecchi went into hiding, Grandi escaped to Portugal and Bottai joined the French Foreign Legion. Between 10,000 and 15,000 rank and file Fascists, most of them connected with the Republic of Salò, became victims of partisan vengeance. The allies and the Rome government pledged themselves to the eradication of Fascism and began a purge of all suspect officials. With its dismal record over the past few years, with no nucleus of effective leaders and with its organisations destroyed, any rebirth of Fascism looked distinctly remote. Anti-Fascism became the rallying cry of the re-emerging parties, enabling Christian Democrats, Socialists and Communists to collaborate with one another in their attempt to re-forge national unity.

As there were several million former PNF members it was soon realised that an extensive purge would be counter-productive, if not impossible. Palmiro Togliatti, as justice minister and leader of the Communist Party, saw the wisdom of calling a halt to judicial proceedings against former Fascists, a view supported by most judges and lawyers, who were themselves in this category! Economic distress, bitterness over the harshness of the peace treaty and general disillusionment quickly created a sense of unease. It was, above all, the coming of the cold war which helped to shatter the anti-Fascist consensus. In 1946 George Kennan's 'long telegram' to the State Department and Churchill's Fulton speech alerted the West to the dangers of Soviet expansionism, the existence of an iron curtain and the presence of powerful Communist Parties in countries like Italy, where they were actually members of a coalition government. This growth of anti-Communism was obviously welcomed by the ex-Fascists. It seemed to offer them the chance of resuming their role as defenders of the nation against the red menace. They were denied this opportunity because the strongest party to emerge after the war was the Christian Democrat Party (*Democrazia Cristiana* or DC) led by Alcide De Gasperi, and it refused to abandon its anti-Fascist principles. After the expulsion of the Communists from the government in May 1947 the DC intended to hold the middle ground against the extremists of the left and the right. It won the support of the urban middle classes in central and northern Italy, the Catholic countryside, the Vatican and the western democracies, and contrived to maintain this pivotal position over the next four decades. This tended to marginalise the neo-Fascists, leaving them very little political space in which to operate.

In 1946 the neo-Fascists were more interested in survival than in political advances. For a time they took refuge within the ranks of an ephemeral protest party called the *Uomo Qualunque* (the everyman party), which won over a million votes in the elections. The referendum on the monarchy which was held at the same time resulted in a two-million vote majority for a republic. Rome and the south of Italy had overwhelmingly supported King Umberto II, and monarchist parties were created to challenge the 1946 verdict. For obvious reasons, neo-Fascists were unlikely to find co-operation with supporters of the House of Savoy a pleasing prospect but they might be forced into an uneasy alliance. A political amnesty granted on 28 June 1946 led Giorgio Almirante and other former officials of the Italian Social Republic to consider founding a new political party, rather than just relyng upon underground groups like the *fasci di azione rivoluzionaria*. On 26 December 1946 the *Movimento Sociale Italiano* (MSI) was established, the word 'social' being a deliberate reminder of the Social Republic of Salò. It has also ingeniously been pointed out that MSI could be read as 'M' for Mussolini and 'SI' for *si*, which, of course, meant 'Mussolini yes'.[1] Almirante led the party until 1951, and then again from 1969 until his death in 1988. The system of proportional representation adopted by Italy in 1946 allowed the MSI, which only polled half a million votes in the elections of 1948 (just under 2 per cent), to return 6 deputies to the chamber (there were 14 monarchists). They secured 29 seats in 1953, overtook the monarchists after 1958, and in combination with them in 1972 won 56 seats (nearly 9 per cent). Their greatest triumph, however, came in the 1994 elections, when they formed the National Alliance with other right-wing groups and joined *Forza Italia* and the Northern League in the so-called Freedom Alliance. They won over 100 seats (over 13 per cent) under their new, young leader Gianfranco Fini. Silvio Berlusconi, the leader of *Forza Italia*, became prime minister and brought the neo-Fascists, but not Fini himself, into the government. The last Fascist ministers had fled from Salò almost exactly forty-nine years before.

So for half a century the MSI had been a constant reminder of the Fascist past, and in April 1994 Fini could refer to Mussolini as the greatest statesman of the century and congratulate Alessandra, the dictator's granddaughter, on her election to parliament.[2] Throughout this period the MSI had drawn most of its support from Rome and the south, from civil servants, university students, retired officers and all those groups who became marginalised during the course of the 'economic miracle' of the 1950s and 1960s. Not all Italians benefited from the rapid growth rate which had been fuelled by the Marshall Plan. While the fate of Trieste hung in the balance between 1947 and 1954, the MSI was able to generate support for a hard line against Tito's Yugoslavia, and even after its incorporation into the republic clamoured for the return of Istria and the other lost territories along the Dalmatian coast. Even so, the neo-Fascists needed to widen the basis of their support. Arguments raged within the party about the tactics and strategy to be adopted. The intransigent activists and the so-called nostalgic Fascists opposed involvement in the political system of the new republic, but the moderates, under leaders like Augusto De Marsanach and Arturo Michelini, advocated participation in the democratic process and electoral pacts with other parties.[3] They encouraged the formation of their own national workers' union (CISNAL), a national welfare association and a students' organisation. The various agencies set up in the Fascist era like the *Opera Nazionale di Maternità ed Infanzia* and *Dopolavoro* had been taken over by the Catholics of the DC and given new names – evidence that the Fascist legacy had its *positive* aspects. Although the neo-Fascists had attacked the regionalism proclaimed in the new constitution (which came into force on 1 January 1948, but was not fully implemented until the 1970s – only Sicily and Sardinia, Val d'Aosta and Trentino–Alto-Adige were initially allowed regional governments) because it threatened national unity, they began to see the possibilities it offered them for consolidating their local power, particularly in Sicily. Their elected deputies and senators in Rome and their councillors in local government were able to use their positions to build up a patronage system. Compared to the operations of the major governing parties – the *partitocrazia* as it was called – the amount of patronage at the disposal of the MSI was negligible, but helps to explain how they managed to survive over the years.

Another reason for this was the presence of friends in high places. Elements within the army, the *carabinieri* (the heavily armed force under the defence minister for military duties and the interior ministry for internal security), the police (under the interior minister), the judiciary, the bureaucracy and in the secret services were sometimes willing to assist the MSI in various ways. To counter the Communist threat the DC and its widespread Catholic network were prepared to accept support from the *missini* (MSI members). In 1960 Prime Minister Fernando Tambroni secured a vote of confidence only because the MSI supported him, but their hopes of government posts were dashed by the public outcry which brought down Tambroni. This set-back and the succession of centre-left coalitions after 1963 led to the revival of the intransigents, some of whom played a part in the projected coup of the *carabinieri* General De Lorenzo in 1964.

By 1969, the year of the Piazza Fontana terrorist outrage in Milan, Michelini and the moderates had to give way to Almirante and a new strategy.

The 'strategy of tension' (terrorist attacks which would prompt an authoritarian response from the government and thus destabilise the DC and Italian democracy) was a consequence of the fears generated by the wave of student and worker protests and the huge anti-Vietnam war demonstrations of 1968–69. Groups which had broken away from the MSI, like Pino Rauti's *Ordine Nuovo* (1956), the *Avanguardia Nazionale* and the *Rosa dei Venti*, were mobilised to meet the Communist threat. Almirante merged his party with the monarchists for the elections of 1972 and won fifty-six seats. This was more than Mussolini had achieved in 1921, but the new *squadristi* were less effective than the old and there was no significant breakthrough, no March on Rome. Another tactic failed. The neo-Fascists joined in the demand for a referendum on the divorce law of 1970, which the church, a majority of the DC and conservative elements wished to abolish. The opponents of divorce lost the referendum of 1974. The DC then turned to the left, exploring an accommodation with the Communists. Once again, the MSI had failed to capitalise on a divisive issue. The party fell into disarray, the strategy of tension appeared to strengthen rather than weaken Italian democracy, and a new generation of right-wing radicals demanded a programme which looked to the future rather than the fascist past. They addressed issues like the environment and the problems of a post-industrial society. After Almirante's death in 1988 Fini and Rauti, the new ideas versus the old, struggled for supremacy in a party which still appeared to be on the margins of political power. The collapse of Communism and the consequent disintegration of the DC – its cohesion being dependent upon a credible left-wing threat – opened up new vistas for the MSI. Without completely severing the links with the past, it called for a new approach to the problems of the 1990s. The old party system with its corruption and mismanagement was totally discredited and had to be replaced. In the elections of 1994 the Italian people confirmed this verdict.

Notes

1 L. Cheles, '*Nostalgia dell'avvenire*. The new propaganda of the MSI between tradition and innovation', in L. Cheles (ed.), *Neo-Fascism in Europe*, London, 1993, p. 50.

2 *The Times*, 2 April 1994.

3 R. Chiarini, 'The *Movimento Sociale Italiano*: a historical profile' in Cheles, *Neo-Fascism*, pp. 28–9.

Selected documents

Document 1

Mussolini often acknowledged his debt to Gustave Le Bon (1841–1931), whose *Psychologie des Foules* was published in 1895 and translated as *The Crowd*. This 'study of the popular mind' described the irrationality of individuals once they became part of a crowd, how 'mental contagion' led to a credulous unanimity and how this process could be exploited by the manipulative skills of masterful leaders and orators. These extracts are taken from G. Le Bon, *The Crowd* (Atlanta, 1982) pp. xiv, 9–10, 20, 34–35, 39, 63, 71, 96, 103, 139.

While all our ancient beliefs are tottering and disappearing, while the old pillars of society are giving way one by one, the power of the crowd is the only force that nothing menaces, and of which the prestige is continually on the increase. The age we are about to enter will in truth be the ERA OF CROWDS.

Different causes determine the appearance of these characteristics peculiar to crowds, and not possessed by isolated individuals. The first is that the individual forming part of a crowd acquires, solely from numerical considerations, a sentiment of invincible power which allows him to yield to instincts which, had he been alone, he would perforce have kept under restraint. He will be the less disposed to check himself from the consideration that, a crowd being anonymous, and in consequence irresponsible, the sentiment of responsibility which always controls individuals disappears entirely. The second cause, which is contagion, also intervenes to determine the manifestation in crowds of their special characteristics, and at the same time the trend they are to take. . . . In a crowd every sentiment and act is contagious, and

143

contagious to such a degree that an individual readily sacrifices his personal interest to the collective interest. . . .

Crowds are everywhere distinguished by feminine characteristics, but Latin crowds are the most feminine of all. Whoever trusts in them may rapidly attain a lofty destiny, but to do so is to be perpetually skirting the brink of a Tarpeian rock, with the certainty of one day being precipitated from it. . . .

Given to exaggeration in its feelings, a crowd is only impressed by excessive sentiments. An orator wishing to move a crowd must make an abusive use of violent affirmations. To exaggerate, to affirm, to resort to repetitions, and never to attempt to prove anything by reasoning are methods of argument well known to speakers at public meetings. . . .

Crowds are too much governed by unconscious considerations, and too much subject in consequence to secular hereditary influences not to be extremely conservative. . . .

The crowd demands a god before everything else . . .

It is tradition that guides men, and more especially so when they are in a crowd . . .

Reason and arguments are incapable of combatting certain words and formulas. They are uttered with solemnity in the presence of crowds, and as soon as they have been pronounced an expression of respect is visible on every countenance, and all heads are bowed. . . .

From the dawn of civilisation onwards crowds have always undergone the influence of illusions. It is to the creators of illusions that they have raised more temples, statues, and altars than to any other class of men. . . .

The hero whom the crowd acclaimed yesterday is insulted to-day should he have been overtaken by failure. . . .

Document 2

On 6 June 1919, two months after their first meeting on 23 March, the founders of the Fascist movement presented their programme. It was very radical but was drastically amended within the next three years. It obviously failed to attract voters because in the elections of November 1919 not a single Fascist was elected to the chamber. The programme is taken from Renzo De Felice, *Mussolini il rivoluzionario* (Turin, 1965), pp. 744–5.

Italians!

Here is the national programme of a solidly Italian movement. Revolutionary, because it is opposed to dogma and demagogy; robustly innovating because it rejects preconceived opinions.

We prize above everything and everybody the experience of the revolutionary war.

Other problems – bureaucratic, administrative, legal, educational, colonial etc. – will be dealt with when we have established a ruling class.

For this WE REQUIRE

For the political problem

a) Universal suffrage with regional *scrutin de liste*, proportional representation, with votes for women and their eligibility for office.

b) Minimum age for votes lowered to 18 years; that for deputies lowered to 25 years.

c) Abolition of the Senate.

d) The summoning of a National Assembly to sit for 3 years, its main task being to establish the constitutional structure of the State.

e) The formation of National Technical Councils for labour, industry, transport, public health, communications etc. to be elected by professional or trade organisations, to have legislative powers and the right to elect a Commissioner General with ministerial power.

For the social problem
WE REQUIRE

a) The prompt promulgation of a state law which sanctions for all workers the 8-hour working day.

b) Minimum pay.

c) The participation of workers' representatives in the technical management of industry.

d) Entrusting these same workers' organisations (if they are morally and technically qualified) with the running of industries or public services.

e) The swift and complete reorganisation of railwaymen and all those in the transport industry.

f) A much needed revision of the draft law on insurance for sickness and old age, lowering the present proposed age limit from 65 to 55 years.

For the military problem
WE REQUIRE

a) The establishment of a National Militia with short training periods and designed exclusively for defence.

145

b) The nationalisation of all arms and munition factories.
c) A foreign policy aimed at enhancing Italy's position in the world through peaceful competition among the civilised nations.

For the financial problem
WE REQUIRE

a) A heavy, extraordinary and progressive tax on capital which would involve a meaningful PARTIAL EXPROPRIATION of all forms of wealth.
b) The confiscation of all property belonging to religious organisations and the abolition of all episcopal revenues which constitute an enormous liability for the Nation and provide a privilege for the few.
c) The revision of all arms contracts and the confiscation of 85% of war profits.

Document 3

Italo Balbo, the *ras* (leader) of the Fascists of Ferrara, emerged as the most formidable and dynamic commander of the blackshirt squads terrorising their opponents in the Po valley in 1920–21. He organised his *squadristi* along military lines and laid the foundations for the Fascist militia. His diary was published in 1932 to mark the tenth anniversary of the March on Rome, and partly perhaps to remind Mussolini of the 'revolutionary' aims of early Fascism with its concern for syndicalism and the plight of the unemployed. He also included Mussolini's speech accepting the monarchy in which the Duce announced his immediate political aims bluntly and simply. The extracts come from I. Balbo, *Diario 1922* (Milan, 1932), pp. 25–6, 51, 63–70, 154–55.

Fascist Syndicalism
26 January 1922
Today at Bologna we established the Fascist Syndicalist Corporations. The order of the day we voted was mine. Thus a great principle triumphantly becomes part of fascist reality: fascism will defend the rights conquered by the workers in thirty years of struggle. It does not matter if false prophets led the people towards false ideals. We will not promise paradise in the future but will offer bread today. The essential thing was to destroy the legend that we are the spearhead of the exploitative egoism of the privileged classes. Fascism is a movement which embraces all Italians

. . . We refuse to give way to the greed of the right just as we resolutely combat the arrogance of the left. For me it has been a marvellous vindication. Last February when I created the first Fascist Syndicalist Unions in the Ferrara region it aroused suspicion. Some accused me of demagogy. As always the most sincere and the most incisive is Mussolini. When he came to Ferrara last spring and was confronted for the first time by a veritable army of workers he remained silent and thoughtful. He speaks of it today in a dramatic article. He thought 'Are they sincere? Will it last? Is it possible?' Yes, it is possible, moreover it is a certainty. The overwhelming reality of today translated into figures gives us a force of half a million organised in fascist syndicalism.

Mobilising the unemployed at Ferrara
25 April 1922
Mussolini assured me that he himself had written to Rome after my warning letters which asked with increasing urgency for the introduction of public works schemes in the Ferrara area. But his letter too had not led to any positive results. I explained my plan to him: suddenly, to bring to Ferrara all the unemployed workers of the province, that is about 60,000 people, mobilising them swiftly before the authorities got wind of it. To occupy the city and not to lift the siege of the Prefecture until Rome gave guarantees of immediate intervention . . . Perhaps the experiment we were about to attempt would be invaluable for the future aims of the revolution. Mussolini did not doubt this and gave his full permission.
16 May 1922
In the morning of 12 May 63,000 people are at the gates of Ferrara . . . At 10 a.m. precisely I rapidly review the columns and put myself at their head . . . The whole city greets our progress. The windows are full. The discipline of these poor peasants with their ragged clothes is splendid . . . The spectators are visibly moved and applaud . . . The castle is blockaded . . . At a given signal, while I pass the doorway, the crowd roars; roars that shake the glass of the surrounding buildings: 'Down with the government, long live Italy'. The noise of countless people is still deafening when I enter the prefect's ante-room . . . Without preamble, speaking with military precision, I deliver the ultimatum 'We will not leave the city until the government sends word and guarantees the concession of public works. We will wait forty-eight hours . . . If this passes without a reply from the government we will begin our action and our first objective will be the prefecture . . .'

The following day
All the public works will be granted . . . We are certain that all our demands have been met. The programme of public works which covers the various zones of the province will be implemented early next week. Victory is complete. I give the order for demobilisation.

Mussolini's Speech on the Monarchy at Udine 20 September 1922
Our programme is simple: we want to govern Italy. We are asked 'Programmes?' But there are already too many programmes. It is not programmes of salvation that are missing in Italy. It is the men and the determination . . . And now we must tackle the problem: how to replace this political class which has always, in the last few years, pursued a policy of abdication when confronted by that wind-filled puppet which is called Italian socialism. I believe this replacement is urgent and the more radical it is the better it will be . . . I believe that the Monarchy has no reason to oppose what we must now call the fascist revolution. It is not in its interests because if it did it would immediately become an adversary, and if it became an opponent it is clear that we could not save it because for us it is a matter of life or death . . . We must have the courage to become monarchists. Because we are republicans? In a certain sense because we see a Monarchy which is not sufficiently monarchical. The Monarchy must therefore represent the historical continuity of the Nation.

Document 4

The Futurists were among the first to support Mussolini and his movement. They had been ardent interventionists and established their own *fasci* to promote their exuberant ideas. Although many of them became disillusioned with fascism, their leader Filippo Marinetti continued to hope that Futurism would become the official art form of the fascist regime. This group of painters, writers, sculptors and architects had burst upon the scene with their Futurist Manifesto of February 1909, published in Paris and designed to challenge the conventionalism of the bourgeois world. Their love of speed, violence and spontaneity won the approval of the early fascists and greatly influenced the 'fascist style'. The extracts from the Manifesto are taken from J. Joll, *Intellectuals in Politics* (London, 1960), pp. 181–4.

Selected documents

Manifesto of Futurism

1. We want to sing the love of danger, the habit of energy and rashness.
2. The essential elements of our poetry will be courage, audacity and revolt.
3. We want to exalt movements of aggression, feverish sleeplessness, the double march, the perilous leap, the slap and the blow with the fist.
4. We declare that the splendour of the world has been enriched by a new beauty: the beauty of speed. . . . a roaring motor car which seems to run on machine-gun fire, is more beautiful than the Victory of Samothrace.
8. We are on the extreme promontory of the centuries! What is the use of looking behind at the moment when we must open the mysterious shutters of the impossible? Time and Space died yesterday. We are already living in the absolute, since we have already created eternal, omnipresent speed.
9. We want to glorify war – the only cure for the world – militarism, patriotism, the destructive gesture of the anarchists, the beautiful ideas which kill, and contempt for woman.
10. We want to demolish museums and libraries, fight morality, feminism and all opportunist and utilitarian cowardice.

It is in Italy that we are issuing this manifesto of ruinous and incendiary violence, by which we today are founding Futurism, because we want to deliver Italy from its gangrene of professors, archaeologists, tourist guides and antiquaries.

Italy has been too long the great second-hand market. We want to get rid of the innumerable museums which cover it with innumerable cemeteries. . . .

The oldest among us are not yet thirty years old: we have therefore at least ten years to accomplish our task. When we are forty let younger and stronger men than we throw us in the waste paper basket like useless manuscripts! . . .

Standing on the world's summit we launch once again our insolent challenge to the stars!

Document 5

The Nationalist Enrico Corradini (1865–1931) was another writer whose ideas influenced Mussolini and the Fascists. In 1910 he was one of the founders of the Italian Nationalist Association and of its mouthpiece *L'Idea Nazionale* in 1911. He supported the

Libyan War (1911–12) and Italian intervention in the First World War. In 1923 he approved of the fusion of the Nationalists with the Fascist Party. As the leading theorist of the Nationalists he popularised the concept of Italy as a 'proletarian nation'. This became a key concept in Fascist ideology. The extract is from a speech he made in January 1914 and can be found in E. Corradini, *Discorsi Politici* (Florence, 1925), pp. 220–1.

There is then a class system in Italy and the socialists proclaim: the system must be revolutionised to elevate the proletariat. Their method of achieving this is strike action. But in Europe there is also a national system and the nationalists proclaim: the system must be revolutionised to elevate Italy and they justify war as the means to achieve this. Referring to the Libyan War the great poet (now dead) Giovanni Pascoli exclaimed: 'the great proletarian has moved'. What did he mean? He wanted to show the similarity between proletarian revolt and that war waged by the humble, patient and inexhaustible motherland of emigrants and workers of the world. Remember what happened next: we were confronted not only by Turkey but by the rest of Europe. Why? What was taking place? What evil had we perpetrated? We had struck at the great bourgeois, the Europe of the bankers, merchants and plutocrats. The great proletarian had attacked the social system of the European nations and they had reacted. The nations of Europe can be compared with the classes within a nation. European nations can be classified and distinguished in exactly the same way that social classes can be identified.

Document 6

Angelo Tasca, expelled from the Communist party in 1929, was an acute observer of the Fascist phenomenon. Writing under the name of A. Rossi his analysis of the rise of Fascism was published before the Second World War and remains one of the best books on this subject. These various extracts are from A. Rossi, *The Rise of Italian Fascism* (London, 1938), pp. 94–7, 103, 263.

Socialist leagues
Out of 280 communes in Emilia 223 were in socialist hands. The landowners, living in town or country, with their sons, their friends, their contractors, and their customers were impotent before the all-powerful workers' syndicates. In the country the

prizes and distinctions of public life were almost entirely denied to the whole *bourgeoisie*, and also to members of the lower middle class who were not members of the socialist organizations. The country landowner who for years had been cock of the walk, head of the commune, manager of all local and provincial bodies, was ousted from all of them. On the land he had to reckon with the 'League' and the employment office, in the market with the socialist co-operative society which fixed prices, in the commune with the red list, which won crushing majorities. Profit, position, power, were lost to him and his children. Hatred and bitterness were welling up, ready at any moment to overflow . . . The old ruling classes felt that they were being swept away to make room for the new social structure. The success of socialist enterprise reminded them daily: *vita mea, mors tua*; and faced with this dilemma, clinging desperately to life, the condemned classes reached by the same logic the conclusion, *mors tua, vita mea*. . . .

Ex-combatants
There were hundreds of thousands of ex-soldiers in Italy, without any special political views, who had gone to the war very young and brought back with them nothing but the memory of their sufferings and their adventures. Why should they turn their backs on such memories when the socialists could give them nothing in exchange? What crime had they committed to turn everyone against them? 'If it is a lie or a piece of sectarian exaggeration', wrote another ex-soldier, 'that the demobilized soldiers have been constantly attacked and abused, it is at least indisputable that we have been shunned, spied on, mistrusted, treated as if we were plague-stricken'. Mussolini was quick to realize the chance offered by the blindness of his enemies. 'The socialists are making a mistake', he said, 'if they believe that those who really fought, that is two or three million Italians, are going to turn round as soon as peace comes and spit on the war in which they fought.' On the contrary, as time went on, and no prospects were offered them, they forgot their suffering, idealized the past, and championed the 'victory' they had won. This state of mind prevailed especially among the officers, that is to say nearly all those members of the middle classes who had taken part in the war.

Squadristi
In the Po valley, the towns were on the whole less red than the country, being full of landowners, garrison officers, university students, officials, *rentiers*, professional men, and tradespeople.

These were the classes from which fascism drew its recruits and which officered the first armed squads. Thus an expedition would usually set out into the country from some urban centre. With arms provided by the Agrarian Association or by some regimental stores, the blackshirts would ride to their destination in lorries. When they arrived they began by beating up any passer-by who did not take off his hat to the colours, or who was wearing a red tie, handkerchief, or shirt. If anyone protested or tried to defend himself, if a fascist was roughly treated or wounded the 'punishment' was intensified. They would rush to the buildings of the Chamber of Labour, the Syndicate, or the Co-operative, or to the People's House, break down the doors, hurl out furniture, books, or stores into the street, pour petrol over them, and in a few moments there would be a blaze. Anyone found on the premises would be severely beaten or killed, and the flags were burnt or carried off as trophies.

The expedition usually had a definite object, which was to 'clean up' a neighbourhood. They would then draw up at once outside the headquarters of the red organization and destroy it. Groups of fascists would round up the 'leaders', mayors, and town councillors, the secretary of the 'league', or the president of the co-operative. These were forced to resign and banished for ever from the district, under pain of death or the destruction of their houses. . . .

Militia

The militia was to become an organic part of the new state, the fascist state. In an article of October 24 the *Popolo d'Italia* foreshadowed its character and functions:

'To the question, what shall we do with the *squadre di combattimento* when we are in power? will they be dissolved? a voice, instinctive rather than rational, answers from the bottom of our heart and says: no, *squadrismo* cannot, must not die. For us it would be suicidal; if force is needed to seize power, it is needed all the more to hold it. The *fascist* militia will be transformed. The squads will cease to be organs of a party and become organs of the state. Transformed by pre-military instruction, they will be the living ideal of the nation in arms. Once *squadrismo* has been militarized the danger of rivalry between it and the other national armed forces will end, as its task will be separate. The volunteer army incorporated in the organization of the new state will be the surest guarantee of the future.'

Document 7

For four years Mussolini had asserted the pre-eminence of the state over the party. These constant repetitions suggest that the message was not being received or was not being believed. This circular was another attempt to confirm the authority of the prefects over all party officials. This document is taken from A. Aquarone, *L'Organizzazione dello stato totalitario* (Turin, 1965), document 42, pp. 485–6.

Mussolini's circular to the prefects 5 January 1927
I solemnly reaffirm that the prefect is the highest authority of the state in the province. He is the direct representative of the central executive power. All citizens, and in particular those having the great privilege and supreme honour of supporting fascism, owe respect and obedience to the highest political representative of the fascist regime and must work under him to make his task easier.

Whenever necessary, the prefect must stimulate and harmonise the various activities of the party . . . The party and its members, from the highest to the lowest, now that the revolution is complete, are only a conscious instrument of the will of the state whether at the centre or the periphery . . .

Now that the state is equipped with all its own methods of prevention and repression there are some 'residues' that must disappear. I am speaking of *'squadrismo'* which in 1927 is simply anachronistic, sporadic, but which reappears in an undisciplined fashion during periods of public commotion. These illegal activities must stop . . . the era of reprisals, destruction and violence is over . . . the prefects must prevent this happening by using all means at their disposal, I repeat by using all means at their disposal . . .

Document 8

One of the classic descriptions of rural Italy under Fascism was written by Carlo Levi in Florence in 1944 and published the following year. He gives a poetic but hard-hitting description of life in Lucania where he was sent in 1933–35 as a punishment for anti-Fascist activities. For most Italian readers it revealed the unknown world of the impoverished south. The extracts are from Carlo Levi, *Christ stopped at Eboli* (London, Penguin edition, 1982) pp. 77–8, 89–90, 132.

The gentry were all Party members, even the few like Dr Milillo who were dissenters. The Party stood for Power, as vested in the Government and the State, and they felt entitled to a share of it. For exactly the opposite reason none of the peasants were members; indeed, it was unlikely that they should belong to any political party whatever, should, by chance, another exist. They were not Fascists, just as they would never have been Conservatives or Socialists or anything else. Such matters had nothing to do with them; they belonged to another world and they saw no sense in them. What had the peasants to do with Power, Government and the State? The state, whatever form it might take, meant 'the fellows in Rome'. 'Everyone knows', they said, 'that the fellows in Rome don't want us to live like human beings. There are hailstorms, landslides, droughts, malaria and . . . the state. These are inescapable evils; such there always have been and there always will be. They make us kill off our goats, they carry away our furniture, and now they are going to send us away to the wars. Such is life!'

To the peasants the state is more distant than heaven and far more of a scourge, because it is always against them. Its political tags and platforms and, indeed, the whole structure of it do not matter. The peasants do not understand them because they are couched in a different language from their own, and there is no reason why they should ever care to understand them. Their only defence against the state and the propaganda of the state is resignation, the same gloomy resignation, alleviated by no hope of paradise, that bows their shoulders under the scourges of nature.

For this reason, quite naturally, they have no conception of a political struggle; they think of it as a personal quarrel among the 'fellows in Rome'. They were not concerned with the views of the political prisoners who were in compulsory residence among them, or with the motives for their coming. They looked at them kindly and treated them like brothers because they too, for some inexplicable reason, were victims of fate.

My sister's visit was quite an event . . . Hitherto the peasants had thought of me as a sort of man from Mars, the only one of my species, and the discovery that I had blood connections here on earth seemed somehow to fill in their picture of me in a manner that pleased them. The sight of me with my sister tapped one of their deepest feelings: that of blood relationship, which was all the more intense since they had so little attachment to either religion or the state. It was not that they venerated family relationship as a social, legal or sentimental tie, but rather that they cherished an occult and sacred sense of communality. A unifying web, not only

154

of family ties (a first cousin was often as close as a brother), but of the acquired and symbolic kinship called *comparaggio* ran throughout the village. Those who pledged friendship to each other on the midsummer night of 23 June and thus became *compari di San Giovanni* were even closer than brothers . . . This fraternal tie, then, was the strongest there was among them.

Towards evening, when my sister and I walked arm in arm along the main street, the peasants beamed at us from their houses; the women greeted us and covered us with benedictions . . . 'A wife is one thing, but a sister's something more'; 'Sister and brother all to one another'. Luisa, with her rational city-bred way of looking at things, never got over their strange enthusiasm for the simple fact that I had a sister . . .

The third of October, which marked the official opening of the war, was a miserable sort of day. Twenty or twenty-five peasants roped in by the *carabinieri* and the Fascist Scouts, stood woodenly in the square to listen to the historic pronouncements that came over the radio . . . The bell-ringer rang out the usual funeral strains, and the war so lightheartedly set in motion from Rome was greeted in Gagliano with stony indifference. Mayor Don Luigi spoke from the balcony of the town hall. He enlarged upon the eternal grandeur of Rome, the seven hills, the wolf that suckled Romulus and Remus, Caesar's legions, Roman civilisation, and the Roman Empire which was about to be revived. He said that the world hated us for our greatness, but that the enemies of Rome would bite the dust and then we would once more tread the Roman roads because Rome was everlasting and invincible . . . Huddled against the wall below, the peasants listened in silence, shielding their eyes with their hands from the sun and looking as dark and gloomy as bats in their black suits.

Document 9

It was only in 1932 that Mussolini, together with Giovanni Gentile, decided to explain the doctrine of Fascism. This article, which appeared in the *Enciclopedia Italiana*, one of the regime's most ambitious cultural projects, rapidly became its most celebrated entry. The extracts are taken from A. Lyttelton (ed.), *Italian Fascisms from Pareto to Gentile* (London, 1973), pp. 41–3, 47, 52–6.

Against individualism, the Fascist conception is for the State; and it is for the individual in so far as he coincides with the State, which is the conscience and universal will of man in his historical existence. It is opposed to classical Liberalism, which arose from the necessity of reacting against absolutism, and which brought its historical purpose to an end when the State was transformed into the conscience and will of the people. Liberalism denied the State in the interests of the individual; Fascism reaffirms the State as the true reality of the individual. And if liberty is to be the attribute of the real man, and not of that abstract puppet envisaged by individualistic Liberalism, Fascism is for liberty. And for the only liberty which can be a real thing, the liberty of the State and of the individual within the State. Therefore, for the Fascist, everything is in the State, and nothing human or spiritual exists, much less has value, outside the State. In this sense Fascism is totalitarian, and the Fascist State, the synthesis and unity of all values, interprets, develops and gives strength to the whole life of the people. . . .

Therefore Fascism is opposed to Socialism, which confines the movement of history within the class struggle and ignores the unity of classes established in one economic and moral reality in the State; and analogously it is opposed to class syndicalism. . . .

Fascism is opposed to Democracy, which equates the nation to the majority, lowering it to the level of that majority; nevertheless it is the purest form of democracy if the nation is conceived, as it should be, qualitatively and not quantitatively, . . .

It is not the nation that generates the State, as according to the old naturalistic concept which served as the basis of the political theories of the national States of the nineteenth century. Rather the nation is created by the State, . . .

Political and social doctrine

Above all, Fascism . . . believes neither in the possibility nor in the utility of perpetual peace. It thus repudiates the doctrine of Pacifism – born of a renunciation of the struggle and an act of cowardice in the face of sacrifice. War alone brings up to their highest tension all human energies and puts the stamp of nobility upon the peoples who have the courage to meet it. . . .

Fascism carries over this anti-pacifist spirit even into the lives of individuals. The proud motto of the *Squadrista*, *'Me ne frego'*, written on the bandages of a wound is an act of philosophy which is not only stoical, it is the epitome of a doctrine that is not only political: it is education for combat, the acceptance of the risks which it brings; it is a new way of life for Italy. . . .

If it is admitted that the nineteenth century has been the century of Socialism, Liberalism and Democracy, it does not follow that the twentieth must also be the century of Liberalism, Socialism and Democracy. Political doctrines pass; peoples remain. It is to be expected that this century may be that of authority, a century of the 'Right', a Fascist century. . .

In the Fascist State religion is looked upon as one of the deepest manifestations of the spirit; it is, therefore, not only respected, but defended and protected. . . .

Document 10

In September 1929 Mussolini relinquished the post of foreign minister and appointed Dino Grandi, who had been acting as under-secretary. As one of the most distinguished Fascist leaders, Grandi's views on foreign policy were keenly awaited. In a speech to the Grand Council on 2 October 1930 he must have surprised many of his listeners by denying the existence of a specific Fascist foreign policy. This extract is taken from Renzo De Felice, *Mussolini il Duce*, i (Turin, 1974), p. 372.

Fascist Italy was the first European nation to establish normal relations with Russia, and that was at a time when smoke was still rising from the ruins of communist establishments destroyed by fascism. This was an act of courage and statesmanship demonstrating that Italy then as now had no intention of subordinating the permanent interests of the nation to any political ideology. Fascism is not – and Mussolini has said this repeatedly – an article for export, nor has it even claimed to be a universal idea or ideology: it is simply an Italian way of life, it expresses the synthesis of our historical experiences and of our specific national needs and aspirations, it is exclusively Italian and it does not expect nor concern itself about other states seeking to imitate it, indeed as fascism is the typical and exclusive expression of the history and civilisation of a specific people no imitation of it can or ever will be a faithful copy of fascism.

Woe to all regimes whose international conduct is based on ideological expansion or on the clash between their own ideology and that of other nations. This inevitably leads to wars of religion and wars of religion as revealed in the sad experience of the 16th century and also in part of the Napoleonic period have soaked Europe in blood . . .

Document 11

Alfred Rocco, lawyer and Nationalist, became one of the main architects of the Fascist regime. As minister of justice (1925–32) he drafted a series of laws enhancing state power. This extract from his report on the Corporations Bill of 16 January 1934 is taken from A. Lyttelton (ed.), *Italian fascisms from Pareto to Gentile* (London, 1973), pp. 295–6.

Report on the Corporations bill

The key body in this new Fascist economy is the corporation in which the various categories of producers, employers and workers are all represented and which is certainly the best fitted to regulate production, not in the interest of any one producer but in order to achieve the highest output, which is in the interests of all the producers but above all in the national interest.

So the state will be making use of individual expertise and self-interest in the higher interests of the nation.

For this reason the so-called self-government of the various groups of producers can perfectly easily be reconciled with state intervention. The self-interest of the producers is not in fact an end but a means, an instrument employed by the state to achieve its own ends, as the representative of the whole collectivity.

This is why the corporations are and must remain state bodies; this does not mean that the state takes over production, any more, incidentally, than it means that the corporations take it over either. Except in special cases where the state takes over directly for important political reasons, as laid down in the Labour Charter, production remains in private hands. The corporations are merely entrusted with the overall control, organization and improvement of production; although state bodies, they are autonomous and composed of representatives of the groups that are themselves responsible for production. The modern corporation is thus very different from the medieval corporation or guild. The latter was indeed a completely self-governing body of producers but it regulated production only in their own selfish interests. The guild existed outside the state and sometimes in opposition to it and it was natural that, being thus enclosed in the narrow circle of its own interests, it ended by stifling productive activity and arousing the hatred of the mass of consumers, thus bringing about its own demise which was greeted with universal acclaim. The Fascist corporation on the contrary regulates production through the producers, not only in their interest but primarily in the interests of all concerned, under the effective guidance of the state. The modern corporation is thus not organized outside but within the state, as a state body. This is certainly how it will act, by utilizing the technical expertise and the individual drive of the producers in order to improve and increase production and made it more profitable, thereby increasing the wealth of the nation.

Document 12

Palmiro Togliatti became the effective leader of the Italian Communist Party after the imprisonment of Antonio Gramsci. Based in Moscow for most of the 1930s, he was a key member of the Third International. Since its birth, Togliatti had been a shrewd observer of Fascism and he lectured on this subject at the Lenin School in Moscow in 1935. These extracts dealing with *Dopolavoro* and corporativism are taken from P. Togliatti, *Lectures on Fascism* (London, 1976), pp. 80–1, 90–1, 101.

Dopolavoro
What do the local *Dopolavoros* do? They carry on a whole series of activities. The benefits the workers have are manifold. They get special terms, reductions for theatre and movie tickets, discounts on food and clothing bought in certain department stores, on outings. Then they also have some form of welfare. In some cases, the *Dopolavoro* tends to take on mutual-aid functions and assists, for example, needy families of disabled workers, etc., etc.

It's time to stop thinking the workers shouldn't engage in sports. Even the smallest advantages are not scorned by the workers. The worker always looks for the smallest thing he can find in order to improve his lot. Just being able to sit in a room and listen to the radio in the evening is something that brings pleasure. We cannot inveigh against the worker who agrees to enter this room for the mere fact that the Fascist symbol is on the door.

We must remember that the *Dopolavoro* is fascism's broadest organization; that our tactics must be broader than elsewhere because, given the way the *Dopolavoro* is set up, we can tie up with broader strata than in other organizations.

Corporativism
Fascism depicts the corporation as the synthesis of two elements: the capitalist and the proletarian. This feature did not exist in the medieval guild. All of fascism's references to the medieval guild are meaningless. . . .

159

In Italy, when the Fascists have spoken and speak of corporativism, they affirm the necessity of class collaboration and the necessity of eliminating the class struggle through collaboration. This is true not only in Italy but in all countries, anywhere corporativism stands out as a means of eliminating the class struggle. Hence, it is readily understood why the fascist unions called themselves syndical corporations at the beginning, even though their nature was entirely different. . . .

But corporativism as class collaboration is not in the least an invention of fascism. It derives on the one hand from the extreme right-wing currents of socialism; petty-bourgeois, anti-Marxist currents that arose within the Second International. . . .

The second origin, or rather the second point of contact, of corporativism as class collaboration is found in Catholic social ideology. You know – and we shall see it more clearly when we speak of the Catholic movement – that in the encyclicals *Rerum novarum* and *Quadragesimo anno* you will find quotations, passages, that correspond to the corporative propaganda of fascism. It's no accident that the Catholic Church and the Vatican substantially accept Italian corporativism. . . .

What is the structure of a corporation? It is based on 'equal' representation of the employers and of the employees, of the technical experts and of the Fascist Party. This 'equality' is only an illusion. As we already have seen, even if the employees' representatives (who are chosen bureaucratically from among the union officials) were truly representatives of the workers, the upper hand would still be given to the bosses by the representatives of the Fascist Party and the technical experts. There is only one president of the corporations: Mussolini. This fact alone shows the predominance of the political factor in the organization of the corporations. . . .

Document 13

Since Cavour's premature death in 1861 no solution had been found to the Roman question. The popes refused to acknowledge the existence of the Kingdom of Italy. Catholics were forbidden to participate in national politics. After 1904 relations between church and state began to improve and some kind of accommodation became a real possibility in the period after World War I. After lengthy negotiation the Lateran Pacts were finally signed on 11 February 1929 by Mussolini and Cardinal Gasparri. These pacts consisted of a treaty, a concordat and a financial convention in which the state indemnified the Holy See for the loss of its territories and properties. This was regarded as one of the great achievements of the Fascist regime. The articles below are taken from J. Pollard, *The Vatican and Italian Fascism 1929–32* (Cambridge, 1985), pp. 197–215.

The treaty

ART. I – Italy recognises and re-affirms the principle contained in the first article of the Constitution of the Kingdom of Italy, March 4th, 1848, by which the Holy Catholic Apostolic and Roman Religion is the only State religion.

ART. 2 – Italy recognizes the sovereignty of the Holy See in the international world as an inherent attribute of its nature, according to its tradition and to the necessities of its mission in the world.

ART. 3 – Italy recognises to the Holy See the full property, exclusive dominion and sovereign jurisdiction over the Vatican as at present constituted, with all its dependencies and dotations, thus creating the Vatican City for the special purposes and with the provisions contained in the present Treaty.

ART. 8 – Italy, considering the person of the Supreme Pontiff as sacred and inviolable, will punish any attempt against him, or the incitement to commit such, with the same penalties decreed for attempts against the person of the King, or incitement to commit such.

ART. 19 – The diplomats and envoys of the Holy See, the diplomats and envoys of foreign Governments to the Holy See, and the dignitaries of the Church coming from abroad to the Vatican City and in possession of passports from the State from which they are coming, visas by the pontifical representatives abroad, will be allowed access to the said City through Italian territory without any further formality.

ART. 21 – All the Cardinals will enjoy in Italy the honours due to the Princes of the blood royal; those resident in Rome, even outside the Vatican City, are to all effects subjects of the same.

During any vacancy of the Pontifical See, Italy will take particular care that the free transit and access of the Cardinals to the Vatican through Italian territory is not hindered, and that no obstacle or limitation is put to their personal liberty.

ART. 26 – The Holy See considers that with the agreements signed today it receives sufficient guarantees for the due liberty and independence of the spiritual government of the dioceses of Rome and of the Catholic Church in Italy and the whole world; it declares the 'Roman Question' definitely settled and therefore eliminated, and recognizes the Kingdom of Italy under the Dynasty of the House of Savoy with Rome as capital of the Italian State.

In its turn Italy recognises the State of the Vatican City under the sovereignty of the Supreme Pontiff.

The concordat

ART. 20 – All bishops, before taking possession of their diocese, will take an oath of fealty to the Head of the State, according to the following formula: 'Before God and his Holy Gospel I swear and promise as is fitting in a Bishop, fealty to the Italian State. I swear and promise to respect, and to make respected by my clergy the King and the Government established according to the constitutional laws of the State. Further, I swear and promise not to take part in any agreement, nor to be present at any meeting, which may injure the Italian State and public order, and that I will not permit my clergy to do so. Desirous of promoting the welfare and the interests of the Italian State I will seek to avoid any course that may injure it.'

ART. 34 – The Italian State wishing to restore to the institution of matrimony, which is the basis of the family, the dignity it deserves considering the Catholic tradition of the nation, recognises the civil effects of the sacrament of marriage as laid down by Canon Law.

ART. 36 – Italy considers the teaching of Christian doctrine in accordance with Catholic tradition, as both the basis and the crown of public education. It therefore agrees that the religious teaching now given in the public elementary schools shall be extended to the secondary schools, in accordance with a programme to be drawn up between the Holy See and the State.

ART. 43 – The Italian State recognises the organisations forming part of the Italian Catholic Action, in so far as, in accordance with the injunctions of the Holy See, they maintain their activity wholly apart from every political party and under the immediate control of the hierarchy of the Church for the diffusion and practice of Catholic principles. The Holy See takes the opportunity of the drawing up of the present Concordat to renew to all ecclesiastics and religious throughout Italy the prohibition to be members of, or take part in, any political party.

Document 14

Except for hostility shown towards Germans and Slavs living inside the northern frontiers, racial questions and anti-semitism were conspicuously absent in Fascist Italy until after the Ethiopian war. Indeed, Mussolini was openly contemptuous of Hitler's racism. All this changed quite dramatically with the publication of the Manifesto of Racist Scientists on 14 July 1938, Mussolini's speech in support on 18 September 1938 and the implementation of these theories with the passage of the Racial Laws in October and November. The brief extracts from the Manifesto and the Duce's speech are taken from Renzo de Felice, *Mussolini il Duce*, ii (Turin, 1981), pp. 866–74 and C. Delzell (ed.), *Mediterranean Fascism 1919–1945* (New York, 1970), p. 177.

Manifesto of racist scientists, 14 July 1938

The concept of race is a purely biological concept. It is therefore based on factors other than the concept of the people or the nation, based essentially on historic, linguistic and religious considerations . . . The population of present-day Italy is of Aryan origin . . . The people of Aryan civilisation have lived in our peninsula for several thousand years . . . A pure 'Italian race' now exists . . . This ancient purity of blood is the Italian nation's greatest claim to nobility. It is time for Italians frankly to declare themselves as racists . . . This does not mean, however, the introduction into Italy of German racial theories as they now exist . . .

The Jews do not belong to the Italian race . . . The Jews represent the only people that have never been assimilated in Italy and that is because they are composed of non-European racial elements, absolutely different from those which produced Italians.

Mussolini's defence of racist policy, 18 September 1938

This speech was, in part, an angry response to Pius XI's assertion that the regime was merely imitating Nazi Germany.

With respect to domestic affairs, the burning question of the moment is the racial problem . . . Those who try to make out that we have simply imitated, or worse, that we have been obedient to suggestions, are poor fools whom we do not know whether to pity or despise. The racial problem has not broken out suddenly . . . It is related to our conquest of our Empire; for history teaches that empires are won by arms but held by prestige. And prestige demands a clear-cut racial consciousness which is based not only on difference but on the most definite superiority. The Jewish problem is thus merely one aspect of this phenomenon . . . In spite of our policy, world Jewry for the last sixteen years has been an irreconcilable enemy of fascism . . . Nevertheless, Jews possessing Italian citizenship who have attained indisputable military or civil merits . . . will find understanding and justice. As for the others, a policy of segregation will be followed. In the end perhaps the world will be more astonished by our generosity than by our rigour . . .

Document 15

On 4–5 February 1939 Mussolini presented his foreign policy objectives to the Fascist Grand Council. He emphasised that Italy would not be fully prepared for war until after 1942 and he made it clear that he intended to concentrate on a Mediterranean strategy. This was the Mare Nostrum concept which he had promoted from time to time over the previous twenty years. This extract is taken from Renzo de Felice, *Mussolini il Duce*, ii (Turin, 1981), pp. 321–2.

The fundamental assumption I am making is the following: that states are more or less independent according to their maritime situation. Those states are independent which possess coastlines on the oceans or have free access to the oceans; those states which do not have free access or are trapped inside inland seas are semi-independent . . . Italy is in an inland sea which is linked to the oceans by the Suez Canal . . . and by the Straits of Gibraltar, dominated by the guns of Great Britain. Italy therefore does not have free access to the oceans; Italy therefore is truly a prisoner in the Mediterranean and the more populated and powerful she becomes the more she will suffer from her imprisonment.

The bars of this prison are Corsica, Tunisia, Malta, Cyprus: the guardians of this prison are Gibraltar and Suez. Corsica is a pistol pointed at the heart of Italy; Tunisia at Sicily, while Malta and Cyprus are a menace to all our positions in the central and eastern Mediterranean. Greece, Turkey and Egypt are states ready to link up with Britain to complete the political and military encirclement of Italy . . . and from this situation . . . we must draw the following conclusions:

1. It is the aim of Italian policy, which cannot have and does not have territorial ambitions in continental Europe, except for Albania, to begin by breaking the bars of the prison.

2. Having broken the bars, Italian policy has just one basic aim: to march towards the ocean. Which ocean? The Indian Ocean through linking up the Sudan, Libya and Ethiopia or the Atlantic Ocean through French North Africa.

In either case we find ourselves confronted by the French and the British. To attempt to solve such a problem without securing our rear in the continent would be stupid. The policy of the Rome-Berlin Axis is therefore the answer to this fundamentally important historical problem.

Document 16

After months of hesitation and increasingly uncomfortable with his policy of non-belligerence, Mussolini finally decided, on 28 May 1940, to intervene in the war on Hitler's side. The startling successes of the German armies in Scandinavia, the Low Countries and France convinced him that he must quickly declare war before it was all over. He informed Hitler on 30 May and gave Badoglio and his chiefs of staff just a few days to make the necessary preparations for a war which he believed the Axis had already won. On 10 June 1940, from the famous balcony on the Palazzo Venezia, the Duce informed the crowd of Italy's declaration of war on Britain and France. These extracts from his speech are taken from Renzo de Felice, *Mussolini il Duce*, ii (Turin, 1981), pp. 841–2.

Fighters on land, sea and in the air! Blackshirts of the Revolution and Legions! Men and women of Italy, of the Empire and of the Kingdom of Albania! Listen! The hour of destiny is striking in the skies above Italy. The hour of irrevocable decisions. The declaration of war has already been delivered to the ambassadors of Britain and France. We are going to war against the plutocratic and reactionary democracies of the West who have invariably hindered the progress and often threatened the very existence of the Italian people . . . Our conscience is completely clear. Along with you the entire world bears witness that the Italy of the Lictor has done everything humanly possible to prevent the blizzard enveloping Europe but all in vain . . . After resolving the problem of our continental frontiers, we are taking up arms to solve the problem of our maritime frontiers; we want to break the chains, territorial and military, which are choking us in our own sea because a nation of forty-five million is not truly free unless it has free access to the ocean.

This enormous struggle is only one phase in the logical development of our revolution; it is a struggle between poor and densely populated proletarian nations and the exploiters who cling fiercely to their monopoly of the world's wealth and gold; it is the struggle of young and fertile nations against sterile peoples falling into decline; it is the struggle between two centuries and two ideas . . .

Italians! In a memorable meeting in Berlin I said that, according to the laws of fascist morality, when you have a friend you stand by him to the end. This we have done and will do with Germany, her people and her magnificent armed forces . . .

Document 17

The invasion of Sicily and the bombing of Rome brought Italy to the brink of collapse. At his meeting with Hitler at Feltre, Mussolini had failed to raise the question of withdrawal from the war. This prompted leading Fascists to demand the summoning of the Fascist Grand Council, which had not met since December 1939. Dino Grandi prepared a motion calling for the transfer of military authority from the Duce to the king. This was supported by a majority of those present, including Luigi Federzoni who much later published his notes of this momentous meeting of 24–25 July 1943 which led to the arrest of Mussolini and the fall of the regime. These extracts are from L. Federzoni, *Italia di ieri per la storia di domani* (Milan, 1967), pp. 284, 291, 201.

Federzoni's summary of Grandi's speech
The Head of Government, Grandi observed, has spoken of the unpardonable errors committed by military leaders and by the armed forces that he himself personally commands. But Mussolini, Head of Government and the minister in charge of all the armed services, has had seventeen years to create, organise, prepare and to select the officer corps, the troops and the equipment. The general staffs that today he blames for the defeat are those that he chose . . . It is now impossible to distinguish between the responsibility of these officers and that of the supreme commander . . . Mussolini today denounces the serious deficiencies of our military organisation. We certainly cannot say that the world war broke out unexpectedly, taking Italy by surprise. For many years the conflict had been predicted . . . Military preparedness was therefore the major task for the man who had the honour of guiding the destiny of the nation . . .

Now is the time for collective responsibility and this is precisely why we judged this to be the opportune moment for summoning the Grand Council. Our order of the day implies that the Grand Council must decide that the regime of dictatorship is over because it has compromised the vital interests of the nation, has brought Italy to the brink of military defeat and has damaged the revolution and fascism itself. The Grand Council must decide to restore all the authority and responsibility of state institutions which the dictatorship has absorbed and return to the crown, the Grand Council, the parliament and the corporations all the tasks assigned to them by our constitutional laws. Above all, it must restore to the crown the prerogative of command, of initiative and of supreme decision-making granted by the constitution.

Federzoni's comments on the meeting
Many people have asked what exactly we hoped to achieve by our initiative. The answer is very simple: one aim only: to secure as quickly as possible Italy's release from the German alliance and from the war. By then we knew that Mussolini was incapable of doing this; it was therefore necessary to force him to leave so that the country would not suffer a complete disaster . . . Now that the invasion of our soil confronted the dictator with the fearful consequences of his leadership and had also shown the most conformist and confused people the undeniable urgency for a change of course, it was possible to attempt such a move with some hope of success; it was up to us to act. It was clear that the king himself needed some formal motive, some constitutional excuse: and, most important of all, only the Grand Council, because it was a fascist institution, would be able to neutralise, as in fact it did, any possible revolt by the party and the militia in support of Mussolini. Our initiative was the only way to spare the country a new and most serious misfortune . . . civil war.

Bibliographical essay

It is obviously unwise to approach the study of Fascist Italy without first acquiring some knowledge of European history in the nineteenth and twentieth centuries. There is no shortage of sound general histories and a useful start can be made by consulting J. Joll, *Europe since 1870*, London, 1973; M. Kitchen, *Europe between the Wars: A Political History*, London, 1988; P. Stearns, *European Society in Upheaval: Social History since 1750*, New York, 1975; and M. Biddiss, *The Age of the Masses: Ideas and Society in Europe since 1870*, London, 1977. These are all in paperback.

There are now an impressive number of works dealing with fascism as a European phenomenon (the 'black cat' of the introduction), and some of the most valuable are E. Weber, *Varieties of Fascism*, Princeton, 1964; S. Woolf (ed.), *Fascism in Europe*, London, 1981; W. Laqueur (ed.), *Fascism: A Reader's Guide: Analyses, Interpretations, Bibliography*, London, 1988; H. Kedward, *Fascism in Western Europe 1900–45*, New York, 1971; S. Larsen, B. Hagtvet and J. Myklebust, *Who were the Fascists? Social roots of European Fascism*, Bergen, 1980; D. Mühlberger (ed.), *The Social Basis of European Fascist Movements*, London, 1987; the *Journal of Contemporary History*, vol. 1, no. 1 (1966) deals with fascism; there is the heavily Germanic E. Nolte, *Three Faces of Fascism: Action Française, Italian Fascism, National Socialism*, London, 1965 and the lighter touch of the Italian maestro R. De Felice, *Interpretations of Fascism*, Cambridge, Mass., 1977. For addicts who read Italian there is also R. De Felice, *Il Fascismo: le interpretazioni dei contemporanei e degli storici*, Bari, 1970.

The difficult but necessary task of exploring the relationship between Fascism and conservatism has been admirably undertaken by H. Rogger and E. Weber (eds.), *The European Right: A Historical Profile*, London, 1965 and more recently by M. Blinkhorn (ed.), *Fascists and Conservatives: The Radical Right and the Establishment in Twentieth-century Europe*, London, 1990 (see in particular the chapter by J. Pollard, 'Conservative Catholics and Italian fascism: the Clerico-Fascists'); the *Journal of Contemporary History*, vol. 13, no. 4 (1978) and vol. 14, no. 4 (1979) deal with 'a century of conservatism' and no doubt prepared the way for Mrs Thatcher.

Progressing from the general to the particular – and some readers may find the journey more exhilarating than the actual destination – there are some excellent books dealing with modern Italy. Three written in English by British historians are outstanding: D. Mack Smith, *Italy*, Ann Arbor, 1959; C. Seton-Watson, *Italy from Liberalism to Fascism, 1870–1925*, London, 1967; M. Clark, *Modern Italy 1871–1982*, London, 1984. For post-1943 Italian history see S. Woolf (ed.), *The Rebirth of Italy 1943–50*, London, 1971; N. Kogan, *A Political History of Post-War Italy*, New York, 1981; P. Ginsborg, *A History of Contemporary Italy: Society and Politics 1943–1988*, London, 1990.

Before listing some of the key books on Fascist Italy, three documentary sources and one historical dictionary must be mentioned: C. Delzell (ed.), *Mediterranean Fascism 1919–1945*, New York, 1970; A. Lyttleton (ed.), *Italian Fascisms from Pareto to Gentile*, London, 1973; G. Bonfanti, *Il Fascismo*, 2 vols., Brescia, 1977; P. Cannistraro (ed.), *Historical Dictionary of Fascist Italy*, Westport, 1982. Cannistraro has put together a remarkable reference book with many entries of article length.

On Fascist Italy, there are two old but short accounts which offer a clear introduction to the topic: A. Cassels, *Fascist Italy*, London, 1969; E. Wiskemann, *Fascism in Italy: Its Development and Influence*, London, 1969. For social and cultural developments an essential work is E. Tannenbaum, *Fascism in Italy: Society and Culture 1922–1945*, London, 1972. More recently the second edition has been published of the excellent A. De Grand, *Italian Fascism: Its Origins and Development*, Lincoln, Nebraska, 1989.

On the origins of Fascism there are two classic accounts by anti-Fascist activists, G. Salvemini, *The Origins of Fascism in Italy*,

New York, 1973 (written in 1942) and A. Rossi, (real name Angelo Tasca) *The Rise of Italian Fascism*, London, 1938. For the various components of the Fascist movement see J. Joll, *Intellectuals in Politics*, London, 1960 (for Marinetti and the Futurists), D. Roberts, *The Syndicalist Tradition and Italian Fascism*, Manchester, 1979, A. De Grand, *The Italian Nationalist Association and the Rise of Fascism in Italy*, Lincoln, Nebraska, 1978 and G. Sabbatucci, *I Combattenti nel Primo Dopoguerra*, Bari, 1974 (war veterans after 1918).

Crucially important for the first years of the regime are A. Lyttelton, *The Seizure of Power: Fascism in Italy 1919–1929*, London, 1973, and A. Aquarone, *L'Organizzazione dello Stato Totalitario*, Turin, 1965. The role of Big Business is covered by R. Sarti, *Fascism and the Industrial Leadership in Italy 1919–40*, Berkeley, 1971, and that of the army by G. Rochat, *L'Esercito Italiano da Vittorio Veneto a Mussolini*, Bari, 1967 with a brief examination of the inter-war years in J. Whittam, 'The Italian General Staff and the Coming of the Second World War', in A. Preston (ed.), *General Staffs and Diplomacy before the Second World War*, London, 1978. For the church, in addition to R. Webster, *The Cross and the Fasces*, Stanford, 1960, there is J. Pollard, *The Vatican and Italian Fascism 1929–32: A Study in Conflict*, Cambridge, 1985.

The most exciting and innovative research has stemmed from the pioneering work by P. Cannistraro, *La Fabbrica del Consenso, Fascismo e Mass Media*, Bari, 1975 (why this was not immediately translated into English remains a mystery) and includes T. Koon, *Believe, Obey, Fight. Socialization of Youth in Fascist Italy*, London, 1985; D. Thompson, *State Control in Fascist Italy: Culture and Conformity 1925–43*, Manchester, 1991; V. De Grazia, *The Culture of Consent: Mass Organization of Leisure in Fascist Italy*, Cambridge, 1981; V. De Grazia, *How Fascism Ruled Women. Italy 1922–45*, Berkeley, 1992.

In foreign policy and imperialism there is A. Cassels, *Mussolini's Early Diplomacy*, Princeton, 1970; C. Lowe and F. Marzari, *Italian Foreign Policy 1870–1940*, London, 1975; the classic F. Deakin, *The Brutal Friendship: Mussolini, Hitler and the Fall of Italian Fascism*, London, 1966 and F. Deakin, *The Last Days of Mussolini*, London, 1966; E. Wiskemann, *The Rome-Berlin Axis*, London, 1966; G. Craig and F. Gilbert (eds), *The Diplomats 1919–1939*, Princeton, 1953; D. Mack Smith, *Mussolini's Roman*

Empire, London, 1976; E. Robertson, *Mussolini as Empire Builder: Europe and Africa 1932–36*, London, 1977; G. Baer, *The Coming of the Italo-Ethiopian War*, Cambridge, Mass., 1967; J. Coverdale, *Italian Intervention in the Spanish Civil War*, Princeton, 1975; R. Quarteraro, *Roma tra Londra e Berlino*, Rome, 1975; M. Knox, *Mussolini Unleashed 1939–1941: Politics and Strategy in Fascist Italy's Last War*, Cambridge, 1986.

For racism, consult L. Preti, 'Fascist imperialism and racism', in R. Sarti (ed.), *The Ax Within*, New York, 1974; G. Bernardini, 'The origins and development of racial anti-semitism in Fascist Italy', *Journal of Modern History*, September 1977; A. Stille, *Benevolence and Betrayal*, London, 1993. For *romanità*, R. Visser, 'Fascist doctrine and the cult of the *Romanità*', *Journal of Contemporary History*, vol. 27, I, 1992. M. Ledeen, Universal Fascism, New York, 1972, is important and so is P. Melograni, 'The cult of the Duce', *Journal of Contemporary History*, vol. II, no. 4, 1976. Also in the same volume of the journal consult M. Ledeen, 'Renzo De Felice and the controversy over Italian Fascism', which arose out of the book by M. Ledeen (ed.), *Intervista sul fascismo*, Bari, 1975.

Anti-Fascism is well covered by C. Delzell, *Mussolini's Enemies: The Anti-Fascist Resistance*, Princeton, 1961.

An interesting and informative way to approach the regime is to read the English translations of Ciano's diaries: *Ciano's Diary 1937–38*, London, 1952; *Ciano's Diary 1939–43*, London, 1947. For a totally different angle read C. Levi, *Christ Stopped at Eboli*, London, 1982 (written in 1944), or the disturbing A. Moravia's *The Time of Indifference*, 1929, or G. Bassani, *The Garden of the Finzi-Continis*, 1962.

Finally, there are biographies and the biggest of all is the multi-volume biography of Mussolini by R. De Felice:

Mussolini il Rivoluzionario, Turin, 1965.
Mussolini il Fascista, i, *La conquista del potere 1921–25*, Turin, 1966.
Mussolini il Fascista, ii, *L'organizzazione dello stato fascista 1925–29*, Turin, 1968.
Mussolini il Duce, i, *Gli anni di consenso 1929–36*, Turin, 1974.
Mussolini il Duce, ii, *Lo stato totalitario*, Turin, 1981.
Mussolini l'Alleato, i, *L'Italia in guerra 1940–43*, Turin, 1990.
Mussolini l'Alleato, ii, *Crisi e agonia del regime*, Turin, 1990.
There is still more to come! In the mean time read D. Mack Smith,

Mussolini, London, 1981. For Balbo see C. Segrè, *Italo Balbo*, Berkeley, 1987; for Farinacci H. Fornari, *Mussolini's Gadfly: Roberto Farinacci*, Nashville, 1971; G. Guerri, *Giuseppe Bottai: un fascista critico*, Milan, 1976; P. Pieri and G. Rochat, *Badoglio*, Turin, 1974; for King Victor Emmanuel and the monarchy see D. Mack Smith, *Italy and its Monarchy*, New Haven and London, 1989. It is most fitting to end this bibliography with a book written by the doyen of British historians engaged in the study of modern Italy.

Index

Acerbo, Giacomo 44, 47, 62, 98
Africa 11, 13, 21, 90, 97, 110–15,
    126–8
agriculture 18, 30–1, 51, 61–2
Albania 104, 119, 127
Albertini, Luigi 39, 43, 49
Alexander, King of Yugoslavia 109
Alfieri, Dino 91–2
Almirante, Giorgio 99, 138–9, 141
Ambrosio, General Vittorio 129
Amendola, Giovanni 49, 53
Anti-Comintern Pact 115, 118
anti-Semitism 95–100, 114, 163–4
Antonioni, Michelangelo 93
apartheid 97
    see also racism
Aquarone, A. 153
arditi 6–7, 15, 19–20, 32
army 9, 44
assassinations 48, 53, 109
    attempts on Mussolini 55, 78
Associazione Nazionale Italiana
    (ANI) 2, 15, 22, 45–6, 149–50
Attolico, Bernardo 120
Augustus Caesar 87, 88
Austria 12, 15–16, 104, 108–9, 114,
    115, 118
Avanti! 8, 13–14, 17
Axis 96, 115–21

Badoglio, General Pietro 26–7, 59,
    109, 112, 121, 123–5, 127,
    130–1
Balabanov, Angelica 12
Balbo, Italo 32–3, 35–8, 40, 44, 49,
    81, 98, 123, 137, 146
Balilla 68–70, 76, 83, 94
Barbusse, Henri 15
Baroncini, Gino 81
Bartou, Louis 109
Bassani, Giorgio 95
Bencivenga, General Roberto 123
Benni, Antonio 39, 51
Berlusconi, Silvio 139
Bianchi, Michele 14, 22, 33–4,
    37–8, 137
birth rate 71–2, 97
Bissolati, Leonida 13, 17
blackshirts 20, 28
Blasetti, Alessandro 93
Blum, Léon 116
Bocchini, Arturo 55–6, 69, 115, 121
Boccioni, Umberto 20
Bolshevism 8, 17
Bonomi, Ivanoe 18, 32
Bontempelli, Massimo 92–3
Bottai, Giuseppe 2, 4, 46, 60, 63–4,
    70, 81, 90, 92–5, 98–9, 107, 129,
    137

Index

Buffarini Guidi, Guido 132, 137

Canaris, Admiral Wilhelm 115
Carnera, Primo 94
Carrà, Carlo 20, 92
Catholic Action 76–7, 78–9
Catholic church 8
  and corporativism 62
  Lateran Pacts 75–9, 160–2
  and Populist Party 19, 34
  and racism 95, 97, 99
  and women and the family 71–2
  see also Pius XI
Catholic university federation
  (FUCI) 77, 78
Cavagnari, General Domenico 125
Cavallero, General Ugo 119, 123,
  129
Caviglia, General 26–7
Chamberlain, Neville 117, 118–19
Charter of Labour (1927) 63
cheka 43
Christian Democrat Party (DC)
  138, 140–1
church see Catholic church
Churchill, Winston 4, 128, 138
Ciano, Costanzo 38, 39, 44, 90
Ciano, Galeazzo 90–1, 102, 114–15,
  119–21, 129, 133–4, 137
Cinecittà 69, 93
cinema 69, 74, 84, 88, 93
Committees of National Liberation
  (CLNs) 131
Communism 2, 138
Communist Party (PCd'I) 8, 19, 31
Confindustria 23, 29, 51, 60, 63, 65
conservatism 29–30, 35, 51
Contarini, Salvatore 101–2, 104,
  106
Conti, Ettore 49
control, social 3–4, 54–7, 66–75
  see also propaganda; terrorism
Corfu 105
Corporations Bill 158–9

corporativism 7–8, 62–4, 159–60
Corradini, Enrico 15, 22, 45, 46, 63,
  102, 149–50
Corridoni, Filippo 14
Cremona 34, 36
Crespi, Silvio 39
Crispi, Francesco 3, 11
Croce, Benedetto 2–3, 83, 85, 91
crowds 3, 110, 143–4
cult of the Duce 4, 59, 87–8, 95
culture, and fascism 82–4

D'Acquarone, Duke 130
Daladier, Édouard 118, 119
D'Annunzio, Gabriele 15, 21–3,
  25–8, 35, 37, 84, 94, 112
De Ambris, Alceste 22–3, 27, 30
De Bono, General 37, 42, 44, 48, 98,
  133, 137
Decennale (1932) 58–60, 88
De Felice, Renzo 144, 157, 163, 164,
  165
De Francisci, Pietro 87
De Gasperi, Alcide 138
De Lorenzo, General 140
Delzell, C. 163
De Marsanich, Augusto 2, 140
De Renzi, Mario 58
De Sica, Vittorio 93
De Stefani, Alberto 50–1, 60
De Vecchi, Cesare 37–8, 39, 69, 70,
  137
Diaz, General 39, 42, 122
Di Giorgio, General Antonino
  122–3
Dollfuss, Engelbert 108–9
Dopolavoro 54, 66, 73–5, 83, 94, 140,
  159
Douhet, Giulio 123
Duce, cult of 4, 59, 87–8, 95
  see also Mussolini, Benito
Dulles, Allen 134
Dumini, Amerigo 43, 48, 53

economic policy 50–1, 60–5
Eden, Anthony 111, 113, 117
education 67–8, 70, 72
Eisenhower, Dwight D. 130
elections 19, 31, 47–8, 56, 141
Enciclopedia italiana 58, 83, 155
Ente Nazionale Assitenza Lavoratori 75
Ethiopia 11, 90, 97, 110–15
Esposizione Universale di Roma (EUR) 86, 119

Facta, Luigi 18, 34, 36–9
family 71–2
Farinacci, Roberto 34–6, 44, 52–3, 82, 92, 95, 97, 129, 132, 137
fasci 6, 17, 31
Fascism
  definition of 1–2, 58
  development of 6–10, 19–23
  ideology 2, 82–3, 155–7
  universal 1, 107–8
Fascist International 1, 107–8
'Fascists of the first hour' 1–2, 6–7, 19–23
Favagrossa, General Carlo 124
Federzoni, Luigi 15, 45, 46, 48, 54, 59, 98, 106, 166–7
Fermi, Enrico 84, 99
Ferrara 36, 147–8
Fini, Gianfranco 139, 141
Finzi, Aldo 43, 48, 96
Fiume 16, 25–8, 106
foreign policy 101–28, 157
  1922–1935 101–10
  Axis 115–21
  Ethiopia 110–15
  Mediterranean strategy 103–4, 122, 125–6, 164–5
  war and defeat 121–8
Forges Davanzati, Roberto 46, 70, 90, 137
France 104–5, 109, 111–13, 119–20
Franco, General Francisco 116–17, 127

Freddi, Luigi 93
Futurism 20–2, 82, 148–9

Gallone, Carmine 88, 93
Gandolfo, General Asclepio 49, 123
Garibaldi, Giuseppe 6, 11
Gasparri, Cardinal 47, 75, 77, 160
General Confederation of Labour (CGL) 18, 32, 44
General Confederation of Syndical Corporations 33, 51
Gentile, Giovanni 1, 40, 46, 48, 67–8, 74, 82–4, 98, 137, 155
Germany 84, 96, 99, 107, 115–21
  see also Hitler
Giani, Mario 73
Gibson, Violet 55
Gide, André 58
Giglioli, Giulio 88
Giolitti, Giovanni 3, 7, 12, 14, 18, 28–9, 31, 34–5, 37, 49
Gioventù italiana del littorio (GIL) 65, 69
Giulietti, Giovanni 27, 37
Goebbels, Joseph 90
Gramsci, Antonio 29, 82
Grand Council 43–4, 56–7, 59, 129–30
Grandi, Dino 32–3, 35, 38–9, 42, 81, 102, 106–7, 113, 117, 129–30, 137, 157, 166
Gravelli, Asvero 107
Graziani, General Rodolfo 110, 126, 127, 132, 134
Greece 104, 105, 126–7
Gruppi universitari fascisti (GUF) 65, 69–70, 72, 77
Guadalajara 117
Guariglia, Raffaele 103, 104

Haile Selassie, Emperor 110
Himmler, Heinrich 115

Hitler, Adolf 108–9, 115–16,
    118–22, 127, 129, 131, 133–4
Hoare, Sir Samuel 111, 113
Humbert, King *see* Umberto

industry 29–31, 51, 60–5
inflation 18, 60–1
intellectuals, fascist 81–5
Interlandi, Telesio 95, 96, 98, 99
Istituto Nazionale LUCE 84
Italian Social Republic 131–3, 137

Japan 115, 126, 128
Joll, J. 148
Julius Caesar 87

Kennan, George 138

Lateran Pacts 75–9, 160–2
Laval, Pierre 109, 110, 111–12, 113
League of Nations 91, 105, 110–12,
    114, 118
Le Bon, Gustave 3, 110, 143
Le Corbusier 58
leisure 66, 73–5
Levi, Carlo 153
Libera, Adalberto 58
liberalism 3, 11, 50–1
Libya 13, 21, 110
Littorial games 70, 72
Locarno Pact 106
London, Treaty of 15, 16, 104
Luchini, Alberto 98
L'Unione Cinematografica Educativa
    (LUCE) 84, 93
Lusignoli, Alfredo 49
Lyttelton, A. 155, 158

Malaparte, Curzio 93
March on Rome 34–40
Marconi, Guglielmo 84
Marinelli, Giovanni 22, 43, 48
Marinetti, Filippo Tommaso
    19–21, 30, 82, 84, 98, 148

Marsich, Piero 36
Mascagni, Pietro 84
Matteotti, Giacomo 48
    murder of 43, 44, 47–51, 53, 82
Mazzini, Giuseppe 20
Mediterranean strategy 103–4,
    122, 125–6, 164–5
Michelini, Arturo 140–1
Militia (MVSN) 9, 44, 152
Minculpop 91, 98
mobilisation 3
monarchy 8, 9
    see also Victor Emmanuel
Montale, Eugenio 94
Montgomery, General Bernard
    128
Montreux congress 1, 107
Morandi, Giorgio 92
Mori, Cesare 44
Movimento Sociale Italiano (MSI)
    139–41
Mussolini, Alessandra 139
Mussolini, Alessandro 10
Mussolini, Arnaldo 107, 123
Mussolini, Benito
    assassination attempts on 55, 78
    and Axis 115–21
    and Catholic church 8, 32, 75–9,
        160
    and coalition government
        38–40, 41–4
    coup against 128–30
    cult of the Duce 4, 59, 87–8, 95
    and D'Annunzio 25, 27–8
    death 134
    dictatorship 56–7
    early life 10–13
    economic policy 60–5
    and education 67
    and Ethiopia 110–15
    and Fascist ideology 1, 4, 8–9,
        58, 82–3, 153, 155
    foreign policy 101–2, 105–10
    and Hitler 108, 115, 118, 120,

127, 129
and industry 29–30
and Italian Social Republic 131–3
and March on Rome 35–40
and Matteotti crisis 47–52
and OND 74
and PNF development 6–10,
    19–23
premiership 39–40, 41–3
and propaganda 84, 89–90
and racism 95–9, 163–4
and Socialist Party 12–14, 17
and Spanish civil war 116–17
speeches 7, 35, 37, 124–5, 148,
    163–4-6
and squads 29–34
and syndicalism 22–3
and terror 3, 17, 81
and universal fascism 1, 107–8
and women 71, 72, 92, 99
and World War I 14, 15–16
and World War II 121–32, 165
Mussolini, Vittorio 93
Muti, Ettore 121

Naldi, Filippo 14
National Fascist Institute of
    Culture 83–4
National Fascist Party (PNF) 2, 7,
    33–4, 37, 54
development of 6–10, 19–23
ideology *see under* Fascism
reform of 42–3, 53–4
and the state 4, 46, 54, 153
National Syndicalists 7
Nationalists Association (ANI) 2,
    15, 22, 45–6, 149–50
Nazi-Soviet Pact 120
neo-Fascism 138–41
Neurath, Baron Konstantin von
    115
Nietzsche, Friedrich 26
Nitti, Francesco 18, 25, 26–7, 34

October Protocols 115
Olivetti, Angelo 14, 22
Olivetti, Gino 51
Opera Nazionale Balilla (ONB)
    68–70, 76, 83, 94
*Opera Nazionale di Maternita e
    Infanzia* (ONMI) 71, 140
Opera Nazionale Dopolavoro (OND)
    54, 66, 73–5, 83, 94, 140, 159
*Opera volontaria per la repressione
    antifascista* (OVRA) 56
Orano, Paolo 22, 97
Orlando, Vittorio Emanuele 16,
    18, 34, 35, 49

Pagano, Giuseppe 86
Paluzzi, Carlo 86
Panunzio, Sergio 22
Pariani, General Alberto 120, 124,
    125
Pavese, Cesare 94
Pavolini, Alessandro 93, 95, 129,
    132, 137
Pelloux, General Luigi 3, 11–12
Perrone brothers 29–30
Petacci, Claretta 72, 134
Pétain, Henri 121, 127
Piacentini, Marcello 86
Pirandello, Luigi 84, 94
Pius XI, Pope 8, 34, 62, 71, 76–9,
    97, 99
podestà 55
Poland 120
police 55–6, 59
Pollard, J. 161
Polverelli, Gaetano 87, 89, 128, 129
Il Popolo d'Italia 6, 14, 15, 22, 37, 92,
    107
Populist Party (PPI) 8, 18–19, 31,
    34, 47
Prasca, General Visconti 127
Pratolini, Vasco 95
press 89–90
Preziosi, Giovanni 95–6, 132, 137

Prezzolini, Giuseppe 13
Pricolo, General Francesco 125
propaganda 88–95
  Decennale 58–60
  OND 74
  racism 98
  radio 84–5
  romanità 87–8
  and youth 66–7
Pugliese, General 38, 39, 45

Quasimodo, Salvatore 94

racism 95–100, 114, 163–4
Radek, Karl 2
radio 84, 90–1
Rapallo, Treaty of 28–9
ras 2, 31–3, 49
Rauti, Pino 141
reform 65–72
  education 67–8, 70, 72
  PNF 42–3, 53–4
  women 71–2
  youth movements 65, 68–70, 76
religion *see* Catholic church
republicanism 8, 9, 20, 131–3
revolutionism 14–15
Ribbentrop, Joachim von 119, 120
Ricci, Renato 68, 69, 132
Roatta, General 115
Rocco, Alfredo 45–6, 52, 54–6, 59,
  63, 158
Romagna 10
romanità 62, 85–8, 96, 99
Rommel, General Erwin 127
Roosevelt, Franklin Delano 128
Rosselli, Carlo 117
Rossellini, Roberto 93
'Rossi, A.' (Angelo Tasca) 150
Rossi, Cesare 14, 22, 43, 44, 48, 49,
  89
Rossoni, Edmondo 22–3, 33, 44,
  51–2, 59, 60, 73
Royal Academy of Italy 84

Russolo, Luigi 20

Salandra, Antonio 15, 34, 35, 38,
  39, 49
Salvemini, Gaetano 35, 64
Sarfatti, Margherita 72, 92, 96, 99
schools 67–8, 70, 72
Schuster, Cardinal 134
Scorza, Carlo 69, 129
Serpieri, Arrigo 62
Serrati, Giacinto 12, 34
Severini, Gino 20, 92
Sforza, Carlo 28, 101
Sironi, Mario 58, 92
Socialist Party (PSI) 7–9, 13, 17–19,
  31, 48
Soddu, General Ubaldo 125
Soffici, Ardengo 93
Sonnino, Sidney 11–12, 16
Spain 116–17, 127
Spinetti, Gastone 107
Spirito, Ugo 60, 64
sport 93–4
squadrismo 2, 9, 28–33, 44, 76, 151–2
Starace, Achille 66, 67, 74, 91, 96,
  98, 114, 121, 137
state
  and the Catholic church 75–9
  and the PNF 4, 46, 54, 153
Steel, Pact of 119
Stresa Front 109
strikes 18, 29, 36, 51–2, 63, 128
student organisations 65, 69–70,
  72, 77
Sturzo, Luigi 8, 34, 47, 76
Suetonius 99
syndicalism 7–8, 21–3, 33

Tacchi-Venturi, Father 77, 79
Tambroni, Fernando 140
Tasca, Angelo (A. Rossi) 150
Terragni, Giuseppe 86
terrorism 3, 17, 32, 34–5, 43, 47–9,
  53, 141

Index

Thaon di Revel, Admiral 39, 42
Tito, Marshal 127
Togliatti, Palmiro 138, 159
Toscanini, Arturo 19
trade unions 18, 33, 51, 62–3
Treccani, Giovanni 83
Turati, Augusto 53–4, 73
Turati, Filippo 34

Umberto I, King 12
Umberto II, King 138
Ungaretti, Giuseppe 94
Union of Soviet Socialist Republics
    (USSR) 107, 120, 127–8, 138
United Kingdom (UK) 104, 109–14,
    117, 120–2, 127–8
United States of America (USA)
    128, 130, 134
university groups 65, 69–70, 72, 77

Valle, General Giuseppe 120, 125
Vansittart, Sir Robert 113, 117

Vecchi, Ferruccio 7, 30
Verona manifesto 132, 133
Victor Emmanuel III, King 9, 15,
    35, 38–9, 48, 50, 56, 77, 130–1
Vidussoni, Aldo 129
violence 3, 17, 32, 34–5, 43, 47–9,
    53
Visconti, Luchino 93
Vittorini, Elio 95
Volpi, Giuseppe 60–1, 65

Wolff, General Karl 131, 134
women 8, 71–2
World War I 9, 14–16
World War II 120–34

youth movements 65, 68–70, 76
Yugoslavia 16, 25, 28, 104, 106, 127

Zangrandi, Ruggero 94
Zaniboni, Tito 55
Zionism 96–7